CW01511618

The A-Z of Inspections in Early Years

Vanessa Dooley

Copyright © 2024
Vanessa Dooley
The A-Z of Inspections in Early Years
All rights reserved.

No part of this publication may be reproduced, distributed, or transmitted in any form or by any means, including photocopying, recording, or other electronic or mechanical methods, without the prior written permission of the author, except in the case of brief quotations embodied in critical reviews and certain other non-commercial uses permitted by copyright law.

Vanessa Dooley

Printed Worldwide
First Printing 2024
First Edition 2024

10 9 8 7 6 5 4 3 2 1

The A-Z of Inspections in Early Years

Table of Contents

Foreword

Following the success of "Are You Ready for Your Inspection?", I was inspired to create a book that would make navigating the world of early years inspections even easier. While the first book provided a comprehensive guide, I wanted to offer something that practitioners could dip in and out of—a resource that would allow you to find exactly what you need, quickly and easily. That's how the idea for "The A-Z of Inspections in Early Years" was born.

This book is designed to be your go-to guide, whether you're preparing for an inspection, reflecting on your practice, or looking for clarity on a particular area. Organised alphabetically, it covers key topics from "Accessibility" to "Zero Tolerance," providing practical advice, clear examples, and actionable tips to help you maintain high standards across your setting.

Inspections are a vital part of early years education—they ensure that children are receiving the best possible care and learning opportunities. But let's be honest: they can also feel overwhelming at times. That's why this book is so relevant. It breaks down the inspection process into manageable sections, offering you the tools and confidence to showcase your setting at its very best.

Whether you're a seasoned manager, a new practitioner, or somewhere in between, "The A-Z of Inspections in Early Years" is here to support you. It's not just about being inspection-ready—it's about embedding best practices that benefit children, families, and teams every day.

I hope this book serves as a go to in your journey to adding impact, making inspections less daunting and your practice even stronger.

After all, we all want the same thing:

Happy, thriving children in safe, inspiring environments.

A is for Assessment

Assessment in early years settings is a cornerstone of quality practice, providing the foundation for understanding children's development, planning meaningful activities and sharing information with parents and other professionals. It's not about endless paperwork but about capturing and using the information that truly supports children's learning journeys. When done well, assessment enables practitioners to see the bigger picture, celebrate children's progress and identify where additional support may be needed. It's a amazing process that evolves as children grow, ensuring they're supported in reaching their full potential. During inspections, assessment is often under the microscope, as it reflects how well a setting knows and meets the needs of its children.

Observations

Observations are the foundation of effective assessment in early years settings. They allow practitioners to see what children know, can do and enjoy, forming the foundation for planning, supporting and extending their learning. The primary purpose of observations is to understand each child as an unique individual. This includes identifying their interests, developmental stage and preferred ways of learning. For example, a child repeatedly engaging with building blocks might be showing an interest in construction or problem-solving. By observing this, practitioners can plan activities that build on this interest, such as introducing more complex construction challenges or linking it to stories about famous landmarks.

Observations also play a key role in identifying any areas where a child may need extra support. For instance, if a child consistently avoids fine motor activities, this could indicate a need to strengthen these skills before they're ready to progress to writing tasks. Early identification ensures that interventions can be put in place quickly, supporting the child's development in a timely manner.

Observations can take many forms, from detailed written accounts to quick snapshots or even photos and videos. Spontaneous observations capture a moment of learning as it happens naturally, such as noting a child's problem-solving skills when building a tall tower during free play. Planned observations focus on a specific area of development, like observing how a child interacts with their friends during group time.

Child-led observations involve watching how children engage with activities they've chosen themselves, which provides insight into their preferences and their core motivation. The real power of observations lies in how they're used. Effective practitioners use observations to inform their planning, ensuring that activities are tailored to the needs and interests of the children. For example, if an observation reveals that a child is fascinated by insects, the practitioner might plan a mini-beast hunt in the garden or create an indoor bug-themed activity.

Progress Checks at 2

The progress check at age 2 is one of the most significant assessments in early years settings, as it provides an opportunity to take stock of a child's development and share insights with parents and other professionals. The progress check is a statutory requirement for children between 24 and 36 months. It involves assessing a child's development in three prime areas: communication and language, physical development, and personal, social, and emotional development. The purpose is to identify strengths, highlight any concerns, and ensure that appropriate support is in place if needed.

Conducting the progress check involves gathering information from various sources, including observations, discussions with parents, and insights from other professionals if applicable. Practitioners should review observations, use the information already gathered to build a picture of the child's development, and speak with parents. Parents are the child's first educators and their input is invaluable. Practitioners should ask about milestones at home, their child's interests and any concerns they may have. The next step is writing the report—a clear, concise summary of the child's development in the prime areas, using positive language to highlight achievements while sensitively addressing any areas for concern. This report should be shared and discussed with parents, ensuring they feel involved and understand the next steps.

If the progress check highlights concerns, such as delays in speech or difficulties with social interactions, practitioners must act swiftly. This may involve providing additional support within the setting, such as focused small-group activities, referring the child to external professionals, like a speech and language therapist, or working collaboratively with parents to create an action plan. Inspectors will often ask about how progress checks are conducted and followed up. Being able to demonstrate that you have robust systems in place, from observations to interventions, shows your commitment to meeting the needs of every child.

Transitions

The transition to school is a significant milestone for children and families and the quality of the transition report plays a key role in ensuring this change is as smooth as possible. A transition report is a summary of a child's development, interests and needs that is shared with their new school or setting. It provides receiving teachers with a clear understanding of the child's starting point, helping them to plan appropriately and build positive relationships from day one.

A good transition report is clear, concise, and comprehensive. It typically includes general information such as the child's name, age, and any key information about their family or background, as well as a developmental overview summarising the child's progress in the prime and specific areas of learning. The report should also include details about the child's interests, preferences, and social and emotional development, along with any information about special educational needs and the support currently in place.

Parents are key partners in the transition process. Discussing the report with parents before it's shared with the school ensures that they feel involved and can provide additional insights. It also allows any concerns to be addressed collaboratively. Inspectors are likely to ask how your setting supports transitions and how information is shared with schools. They'll want to see that your reports are thorough, child-centred and supportive of continuity in learning and care.

Assessment isn't just about meeting statutory requirements—it's a powerful tool for improving practice and outcomes for children. Regularly reviewing assessment data can help identify patterns and trends, such as areas of learning where children may need more support. For example, if several children are struggling with fine motor skills, this could prompt a review of the activities and resources available in your setting. Assessment data can also highlight areas for staff development. For instance, if observations reveal that practitioners are less confident in supporting mathematical development, targeted training can address this gap. Sharing assessment information with parents helps build strong partnerships. Inviting parents to contribute to learning journeys or offering workshops on supporting learning at home makes assessment a collaborative process.

During inspections, assessment is a key focus, as it reflects how well a setting understands and supports the children in its care. Inspectors will want to see that assessment is embedded in your practice, not treated as an add-on. Be prepared to explain how observations inform planning and support individual needs, how progress checks and transition reports are conducted and followed up, and how assessment data is used to evaluate and improve your setting.

Organisation is key

Having clear, well-organised evidence helps demonstrate your approach. This might include examples of learning journeys that show progress over time, copies of recent progress checks and transition reports, and action plans for children identified as needing additional support. Inspectors may also ask staff about their role in assessment, so ensure your team is confident in explaining how they observe, assess, and plan for children's learning. Regular training and reflective discussions can help build this confidence.

Assessment in early years settings is about much more than meeting statutory requirements—it's about understanding, supporting, and celebrating each child's unique journey. Through thoughtful observations, robust progress checks, and meaningful transition reports, practitioners can ensure that every child has the best possible start in life. For inspections, strong assessment practices demonstrate your setting's commitment to quality and continuous improvement.

By embedding assessment into daily routines, engaging families and using the information to enhance practice, you create a setting where children thrive and inspectors can clearly see the impact of your efforts.

B is for Behaviour Management

Encouraging Positive Behaviour Through Understanding

In an early years setting, behaviour isn't something we "control" or "fix"—it's something we nurture, guide and support. Positive behaviour grows when children feel secure, valued as well as and understood. It's about looking beyond the surface of their reactions to understand what they are trying to communicate. By focusing on connection and encouraging positive behaviour, we are then able to help children develop the social-emotional skills they'll carry with them for life.

Everything starts with relationships.

Positive behaviour is rooted in how children feel about the adults and peers around them. When children feel safe, valued and genuinely cared for, they are more likely to express positive behaviours. As practitioners, it's our role to create a warm, nurturing environment where children feel comfortable being themselves. It is up to us to be able to promote this in everyday practice.

Building trust begins with simple, consistent responses. Warm smiles, engaging conversations as well as taking the time to listen show children that they matter. When children feel they are truly seen and heard, they are less likely to act out in frustration or seek attention through negative behaviours.

Relationships also form the foundation for teaching emotional safety. Emotional literacy is a key skill we can nurture in early years settings. Helping children name and understand their feelings gives them the tools to express themselves constructively. Simple strategies like using a feelings chart or reading books about emotions can help children recognise and articulate what's going on inside them. Phrases like "It's okay to feel upset" or "Can you show me how you're feeling with this chart?" validate their emotions and show them that all feelings are acceptable—it's how we respond to them that matters. Another good example of recognising emotions is "Name it Tame it". Being able to name the emotion children are experiencing then being able to use strategies to tame it to get a result.

Being a Role Model

Let's be honest: Little eyes are always watching. Children learn a great deal by observing the adults around them. The way we speak, act, and respond sets the tone for the behaviours we want to see. If we approach situations calmly, speak kindly and treat others with empathy, children will naturally mirror these actions.

This doesn't mean we need to be perfect—after all, we're only human! If we make a mistake, like raising our voice in frustration, it's an opportunity to model how to apologise and repair a relationship. Saying, "I'm sorry I spoke loudly. I was feeling frustrated, but I shouldn't have done that," teaches children the importance of accountability and forgiveness.

Fostering Positive Social Interactions

Social interactions can be tricky for young children, especially when sharing, turn-taking or disagreements are involved. Our role is to guide children through these moments, helping them build the skills they need to interact positively with others.

Rather than focusing on what children shouldn't do, highlight the behaviours you *do* want to see. For example, instead of saying, "Don't snatch," you could say, "Let's take turns; it's your friend's turn first, and then it will be yours." This shifts the focus to a solution and reinforces positive actions.

Praise is a powerful tool for encouraging behaviour. A simple "I noticed you helped your friend tidy up—thank you, that was kind," goes a long way in reinforcing positive actions. Specific praise helps children understand exactly what they've done well, making it more likely they'll repeat it.

While praise is important, rewards can also be helpful in moderation. For example, a group reward system, like adding marbles to a jar for cooperative behaviour, can encourage teamwork and shared goals. Once the jar is full, the group can enjoy a special activity, like an outdoor picnic or a storytelling session just as an example.

Guiding Self-Regulation

Ultimately, behaviour management is about helping children learn to regulate their own emotions and actions. This doesn't happen overnight—it's a skill that takes time, patience, and lots of support to develop. We see and hear so many practitioners who say "oh we tried that" But remember Rome was not built in a day and it needs to be consistently done to achieve the results you want.

One of the most effective ways to teach self-regulation is through problem-solving. When a child struggles with sharing, instead of stepping in with a solution, guide them through the process. Ask questions like, "How do you think your friend feels when you take the toy? What could we do instead?" These conversations help children understand the impact of their actions and encourage empathy.

Transitions can also be a challenge for many children. Whether it's moving from being outdoors to snack time or tidying up to go outside, transitions often disrupt a child's sense of control. Tools like visual timers, countdowns, or transition songs can make these moments smoother. Giving children a heads-up—"In five minutes, we'll tidy up"—helps them prepare for the change.

Choice is another powerful tool for supporting behaviour. By offering children two options, such as "Would you like to sit on the carpet or the cushion for storytime?" you empower them to feel in control while still guiding their actions. We have seen this work so many times. Children then feel they are in control of their behaviour and their emotions as they have made the choice.

Creating a Positive Environment

The environment plays a huge role in shaping children's behaviour. A calm, organised space helps children feel secure and focused. Ensure there are clearly defined areas for different activities—such as a cosy reading corner, a space for creative play, and an area for quiet time.

Having a quiet or sensory-friendly space is particularly helpful for children who might become overwhelmed. These areas can include soft cushions, calming colours and sensory toys, providing a place for children to reset and regulate their emotions.

Routine is another important factor. While flexibility is essential in early years, having a predictable routine gives children a sense of stability and security. It also helps us as practitioners too! When children know what to expect, they are more likely to feel confident and in control of their day.

Recognising Individual Needs

Every child is different and their behaviour reflects their unique character, experiences and developmental stage. Some children may need additional support, such as sensory aids, visual schedules or one-on-one guidance, to feel successful.

It's important to remember that behaviour is a form of communication. A child who is "having a wobble" may be telling you they're tired, overwhelmed or in need of connection. Taking the time to observe and understand the "why" behind a behaviour allows you to respond in a way that truly supports the child.

Partnering With Families

Families are an invaluable part of the behaviour management process. Building open, honest communication with parents ensures that everyone is working together to support the child. Share successes, no matter how small, and celebrate milestones together.

It's also helpful to provide families with strategies they can use at home. For example, if visual timetables or emotion charts work well in your setting, share this with parents so they can create consistency across environments.

Workshops or parent information sessions can also be a great way to empower families. By helping parents understand their child's behaviour and providing them with tools to support positive actions, you create a unified approach that benefits the child. This is also great collaboration with parents.

Encouraging Growth Through Connection

Behaviour management in early years isn't about enforcing rules or controlling children—it's about building relationships, creating safe spaces, and helping children develop the skills they need to navigate the world. By focusing on connection, guidance, and understanding, we can foster a setting where every child feels valued and empowered to make good choices.

Positive behaviour isn't the end goal; it's a natural outcome of an environment that prioritises empathy, support, and growth. When we nurture these values in our settings, we're not just helping children today—we're giving them the tools to thrive for a lifetime.

C is for Communication

The Foundation of a Thriving Early Years Setting

Communication lies at the heart of every successful early years setting. It's the glue that binds relationships between children, parents and staff to create a harmonious environment where everyone feels valued, connected as well as supported. Effective communication isn't just about exchanging information; it's about fostering trust, building understanding, and creating a shared sense of purpose.

When communication is prioritised, children's needs are better understood, parents feel engaged and confident and staff work collaboratively to achieve shared goals. It's this foundation that allows the entire setting to thrive.

In our interactions with children, communication goes far beyond words. We need to remember this.

Young children are still developing their language skills, so they often rely on non-verbal cues—such as facial expressions, gestures, or behaviours—to express themselves. As practitioners, it's our role to actively listen and observe, making sense of these signals with care and empathy.

Listening with our full attention—getting down to their level, making eye contact, and showing genuine interest—demonstrates that we value their thoughts and feelings. This not only strengthens their trust in us but also supports their emotional security and confidence.

Using age-appropriate language is key when communicating with children. Simple words and clear, short sentences help them understand what's being said, while repetition reinforces learning.

For instance, saying "Time to tidy up" each day before cleanup provides consistency, helping children associate the phrase with the action. Visual aids, such as picture cards, timetables and sign language, can further bridge communication gaps, particularly for non-verbal children, those with speech delays, or children learning English as an additional language.

A visual timetable, for example, helps children understand the routine of the day, reducing uncertainty and promoting a sense of control. Encouraging children to express themselves—whether through words, gestures, drawings, or role-play—fosters self-expression and builds confidence. Recognising and celebrating their efforts, even when words aren't clear, shows them their voice matters. This is so important in our sector.

Strong communication with parents is equally as vital. Parents are their child's first and most important educators and their insights are invaluable in shaping how we support their children. Daily interactions at drop-off and pick-up provide opportunities for quick but meaningful exchanges, like sharing a small achievement from the day.

For example, a simple "Jack worked so hard on building a tall block tower today" can brighten a parent's day and strengthen their connection with the setting. Beyond daily chats, regular updates through newsletters, emails, or communication apps keep parents informed about their child's progress and the setting's activities. Sharing photos and anecdotes allows parents to feel part of their child's journey, even when they can't be there.

Parent-practitioner meetings offer a more focused space for discussing a child's development. These should always be a two-way conversation, inviting parents to share insights from home and collaboratively set goals. Approaching these discussions with openness and positivity builds trust and reinforces the sense of partnership.

Engaging parents in the setting's activities can further strengthen relationships. Stay-and-play sessions, cultural celebrations, or workshops offer parents the chance to be part of their child's world and contribute to the community. Such involvement not only enriches the children's experiences but also demonstrates to parents that their input is valued. When sensitive conversations, such as developmental concerns or behavioural challenges, need to happen, empathy is crucial. Choosing a private, calm setting and focusing on shared goals for the child helps ensure these discussions are constructive and supportive.

Communication within the staff team is just as important as with children and parents. A well-connected team ensures consistency in practice and a shared understanding of each child's needs. Regular team meetings provide a platform to share updates, successes, and challenges, fostering collaboration and a sense of collective responsibility. These meetings can also support professional growth, with staff sharing ideas, insights, and strategies from training. Maintaining clear documentation, such as observation notes and learning plans, ensures that all staff are informed and able to provide consistent care, even during transitions or staff absences.

Open communication channels within the team create a supportive work culture. Encouraging staff to share ideas, voice concerns, or ask questions without fear of judgment promotes a positive atmosphere. This can be achieved through open-door policies, suggestion boxes, or regular one-on-one check-ins with leadership. When staff feel heard and valued, their job satisfaction increases, which positively impacts their interactions with children and parents. Leadership also plays a vital role in modelling effective communication and resolving any conflicts that may arise. Addressing misunderstandings promptly and respectfully ensures that they don't escalate, preserving a healthy team dynamic.

Creating a culture of effective communication requires intentionality.

Inclusivity is key

Ensuring that all families and staff can access and engage with communication methods. This might mean translating materials for non-English-speaking families, using simple language, or providing alternative formats like audio recordings. For staff or children with communication difficulties, adapting methods, such as using sign language or assistive technologies, demonstrates a commitment to inclusivity.

Encouraging feedback from parents and staff also strengthens communication. Whether through surveys, suggestion boxes, or informal chats, listening to feedback and acting on it where possible shows that everyone's voice matters. Embracing the diversity of families and staff by incorporating different cultures and traditions into the setting further enhances inclusivity and enriches the environment.

While communication barriers can arise, they can often be overcome with proactive strategies. Language differences, for instance, can be addressed with visual aids or translation services. Time constraints can be mitigated with flexible meeting options or unscheduled communication methods, like recorded video updates. Emotional barriers, such as stress or anxiety, can be eased through empathetic and non-judgmental interactions. By remaining flexible and patient, we can navigate these challenges and maintain strong connections.

When communication is prioritised, the benefits ripple throughout the setting.

For children, clear and consistent communication supports their learning, emotional well-being, and relationships. They feel heard, understood, and confident to express themselves.

For parents, open communication builds trust and strengthens their engagement in their child's education, providing reassurance that their child's needs are being met.

For staff, effective communication fosters teamwork, reduces misunderstandings, and enhances job satisfaction, creating a positive and productive work environment.

Ultimately, communication is the foundation upon which a thriving early years setting is built. It connects everyone—children, parents, and staff—in a shared commitment to the well-being and development of every child. Whether through words, gestures, or actions, every interaction is an opportunity to strengthen these bonds and create a setting where everyone feels valued, supported and just as important to feel empowered to succeed.

D is for Documentation

The Backbone of Accountability and Excellence

In an early years setting, documentation isn't just paperwork that sits on a shelf—it's the backbone of everything we do. It's a powerful tool for tracking children's development, showing how we meet their needs, and proving that we're running a safe, high-quality setting. Done well, documentation keeps us organised, reflective, and ready for anything—whether it's an inspection, a conversation with parents, or planning next steps for a child's learning journey.

Children's Learning and Development Records

At the heart of our documentation are the records of children's learning and development. These aren't just about ticking boxes; they tell the story of each child's unique journey with us. Observations, assessments, and planning are central to this process, helping us tailor activities and experiences that meet their developmental needs and interests.

Observations are where we capture those wonderful, everyday moments of learning—whether it's a child experimenting with colours at the art table, working out how to balance a tower of blocks, or figuring out how to share a toy with a friend. These snapshots give us insights into what the child is learning and enjoying. But it's not just about noting what's happening; it's about digging deeper to understand the *why*.

Why is this activity capturing their attention?

What skills are they practising?

What could we do to extend this interest?

Assessments help us piece these observations together, showing how children are progressing in relation to the Early Years Foundation Stage (EYFS) framework. They highlight what's going well and where we might need to offer extra support. For example, if a child is struggling with fine motor skills, our documentation helps us spot this early and plan activities to strengthen those abilities, like threading beads or playing with playdough.

Planning completes the cycle, turning our observations and assessments into meaningful actions.

A well-documented plan shows that we're responding to the child's interests and needs. If a child is fascinated by insects, for instance, we might plan a bug hunt or set up a nature table with magnifying glasses and insect models. This connection between documentation and practice is something inspectors love to see, as it proves that we're not only observing but actively supporting children's learning.

Policies and Procedures

Policies and procedures are the backbone of how we run the setting—they outline what we stand for, how we operate, and how we keep everyone safe. From safeguarding and behaviour management to health and safety and inclusion, these documents are our go-to guides for handling daily routines and unexpected challenges.

But having policies isn't enough—they need to be clear, up-to-date, and accessible.

Regularly reviewing them ensures they reflect current guidance and the realities of day-to-day practice. For example, your safeguarding policy should clearly state how concerns are reported, who is responsible, and how children are protected from harm. During inspections, these policies provide evidence that your setting is well-organised, consistent, and professional. Also ensure the dates from legislation is updated constantly.

Parents also benefit from clear policies. Whether it's a quick reference in a parent handbook or a display on the noticeboard, these documents reassure families that their children are in capable hands. A well-written positive behaviour policy, for example, shows parents how we approach challenges with empathy and consistency, fostering trust and understanding.

Safeguarding and Health & Safety Records

Safeguarding is non-negotiable, and the documentation that supports it must be meticulous. From staff training logs and DBS checks to incident reports, these records prove that child safety is always our top priority. When safeguarding concerns arise, having a clear, well-maintained record of what happened, who was informed and the actions taken shows accountability and professionalism.

Health and safety documentation is equally important. Regular risk assessments, daily safety checks, and accident logs demonstrate that we're actively creating a safe environment for children. Whether it's checking outdoor equipment or ensuring first aid supplies are stocked, these small but vital tasks keep everyone safe and show inspectors that we take our responsibilities seriously.

Parent Communication and Engagement

Parents are the first and most important educators in a child's life, so keeping them involved is essential. Good communication is the foundation of these relationships, and documenting this interaction helps us track how we're working together to support the child.

Daily handovers are often where these conversations start. Sharing a quick update about their child's day—like how they enjoyed painting or played with friends—helps parents feel connected. For more formal updates, we might use learning journals, progress reports, or newsletters. These give parents a deeper understanding of their child's development and keep them in the loop about what's happening in the setting.

It's also important to document any discussions with parents about their child's needs, progress, or concerns. For example, if a parent mentions that their child is struggling to sleep at night, making a note ensures that everyone on the team is aware and can offer extra support, like a calm, quiet space for rest during the day. Inspectors often look for evidence of parent engagement, and having records of newsletters, meeting minutes, and parent feedback demonstrates how we involve families in their child's learning.

Self-Evaluation and Continuous Improvement

Being inspection-ready isn't just about having the right records; it's about showing that we're always striving to improve. This is where self-evaluation comes in. A Self-Evaluation Form (SEF) is a great way to reflect on what's working well and identify areas for growth. It's like holding a mirror up to your practice and asking, "How can we do even better?" or using floor books demonstrating that you do well, the impact and what you can do better. If you are wanting help with this please contact us regarding our #Justquality Accreditation on admin@jigsaweyc.com.

Action plans are a practical way to turn self-evaluation into progress. Whether it's enhancing the outdoor area, introducing new training for staff, or improving resources for children with additional needs, documenting these goals shows that we're proactive and committed to raising standards. For example, if you identify that children need more opportunities for physical play, an action plan might include purchasing climbing equipment or organising outdoor movement sessions.

Staff appraisals and training records are also vital. They show that we're investing in our team's development, which directly benefits the children. Regular training on topics like safeguarding or behaviour management ensures that staff are confident and up-to-date with best practices.

Staying Organised for Inspections

When it comes to inspections, being well-organised can make all the difference. Inspectors want to see clear, accessible documentation that reflects your setting's strengths and compliance. This doesn't mean drowning in paperwork—it's about keeping everything in its place, current and easy to find.

Using digital platforms or a well-structured filing system can save time and reduce stress. For instance, having a folder for each child's learning journey, a centralised log for safeguarding records, and clearly labelled policy documents ensures you can access what you need quickly. Regularly auditing your records helps catch any gaps or updates that might be needed, so you're always inspection-ready.

The Benefits of Strong Documentation

Good documentation isn't just about ticking boxes for inspectors—it's about making life easier for everyone. For children, it ensures their progress is tracked, celebrated, and supported. For parents, it provides transparency, reassurance, and a sense of partnership. For staff, it brings clarity and consistency, making the setting run smoothly and efficiently.

Documentation also protects the setting. If concerns ever arise, whether from parents, staff, or inspectors, having detailed records provides a clear account of events and decisions. It's a safeguard that ensures transparency and professionalism.

E is for Environment

Creating a Stimulating, Safe, and Nurturing Space for All Children

The environment in an early years setting is so much more than a backdrop; it's an active part of the learning process. The space, resources, and atmosphere we create have a direct impact on how children feel, play, and learn. A well-thought-out environment sparks curiosity, promotes exploration as well as supporting independence. At the same time, it must feel safe, welcoming and inclusive—a space where every child feels they belong.

An effective early years environment isn't static; it grows and adapts with the children, meeting their diverse needs and evolving interests. Whether indoors or out, every corner of the setting has the potential to inspire learning and nurture well-being.

Physical Environment: Safe and Stimulating

Safety is non-negotiable.

Before anything else, an environment must be a secure place where children can explore confidently. Regular risk assessments are a key part of this, ensuring that potential hazards are addressed promptly. Think soft flooring in areas where children might tumble, child-sized furniture to support independence, and secure gates to keep little ones safe during outdoor play. A safe environment doesn't stifle exploration or investigation—it creates a foundation where children can test their boundaries without unnecessary risk.

Once safety is in place, the focus can shift to creating a space that invites children to play and learn. A warm, welcoming environment is one where children feel at home. Natural light, soft colours, and a mix of textures can help create a calming atmosphere, while thoughtful organisation allows children to explore independently. Open shelving, for instance, lets children access resources easily, empowering them to make choices and follow their interests.

Dividing the space into zones for different activities provides both structure and variety. A cosy reading corner with cushions and books creates a quiet retreat, while a role-play area stocked with costumes and props invites imaginative adventures. Sensory play areas, complete with water trays or textured objects, give children the chance to explore with their senses, while an art zone filled with paints, paper, and other materials encourages creativity. Each area should feel purposeful and accessible, sparking curiosity and supporting development in different ways.

Outdoor Environment: A World of Discovery

The outdoors is a treasure trove of learning opportunities, and your outdoor space should be just as carefully considered as your indoor environment. Outdoor play supports physical development, encourages risk-taking, and connects children with the natural world. It's a space where they can run, climb, dig, and discover—all while building confidence and resilience.

Incorporating natural elements into outdoor play areas makes the experience even richer. Sand, water, mud, and plants invite sensory exploration and scientific discovery. A mud kitchen, for example, allows children to engage in pretend play while also getting hands-on with nature. A simple garden bed can become a hub of activity, from planting seeds to observing insects.

It's also important to make outdoor spaces usable in all weather. Waterproof clothing and wellies allow children to splash in puddles or explore damp grass, while sheltered areas provide protection from rain or too much sun. An all-weather approach ensures children can benefit from outdoor play year-round, building a strong connection with the environment and the changing seasons.

Inclusive and Adaptable

A great early years environment works for every child, no matter their abilities or needs. Inclusivity isn't an add-on; it's woven into the design of the space. Accessible features like ramps, wide walkways, and appropriately designed facilities ensure that children with mobility challenges can navigate the setting easily.

For children with sensory sensitivities, quiet corners or sensory-friendly spaces provide a retreat where they can self-regulate. These areas might include soft lighting, calming colours, and tactile resources like weighted blankets or textured toys.

An adaptable environment is also key. Children's interests and developmental stages are always evolving, so the space needs to evolve with them. Rotating resources, rearranging areas, or introducing new materials keeps the environment fresh and engaging. For instance, if children develop a fascination with transport, a role-play area can quickly become a garage or train station. Flexibility shows children that their interests are valued and keeps learning exciting.

Resources and Materials

The resources and materials in your setting play a huge role in shaping children's experiences. Open-ended resources are particularly valuable, as they encourage creativity, critical thinking, and problem-solving. Blocks, loose parts like shells or wooden rings, and art materials allow children to explore and invent without the limitations of a set purpose.

It's equally important that resources reflect the diversity of the children in your setting.

Books, toys, and displays should represent different cultures, languages, and family structures, fostering a sense of belonging and respect for others. For example, dolls with different skin tones, books featuring various family dynamics, and music from around the world create an inclusive environment where every child feels seen and valued.

Developmentally appropriate resources are another essential consideration.

Younger children may need simpler tools or larger items that are easier to manipulate, while older children might thrive with more complex challenges. Providing a mix ensures that every child can engage with the environment at their own level.

Emotional Environment: A Space for Well-Being

The physical environment is only part of the balance; the emotional environment is just as important.

Children need to feel safe, respected, and supported to fully engage in their learning.

Creating a nurturing atmosphere starts with building strong, positive relationships. When children know they're listened to and their feelings are valued, they develop a sense of trust and belonging. Small, everyday actions—like getting down to their level when speaking or acknowledging their emotions—help create this supportive atmosphere.

An environment that promotes independence also boosts emotional well-being. When children are given the freedom to make choices, take risks, and try new things, they develop confidence and a sense of agency. Simple adjustments, like storing materials at child height or using visual prompts, can empower children to take ownership of their play and learning.

Supporting Learning Through the Environment

In early years settings, the environment is often referred to as the "third teacher," after adults and peers. The way the space is set up can shape how children learn, play, and interact. A well-designed environment acts as an active participant in the learning process, offering provocations and invitations to explore.

Provocations are thoughtfully arranged resources or activities that spark curiosity and encourage deeper thinking. For example, placing a selection of autumn leaves, magnifying glasses, and paper for drawing nearby might prompt children to explore colours, shapes, and textures. Similarly, a construction area stocked with unusual materials like corks, spools, and pipes invites experimentation and problem-solving.

Displays can also play a significant role in supporting learning. Showcasing children's work at their eye level gives them a sense of pride and ownership. Whether it's a wall filled with their artwork, a collection of photos capturing recent activities, or a project board documenting group learning, these displays make learning visible to children, parents, and inspectors alike.

Preparing the Environment for Inspections

Your environment speaks volumes about your approach to early years education, and during an inspection, it's one of the first things inspectors will notice. A well-organised, clean, and stimulating space demonstrates that you've put thought and care into creating an environment that supports children's development.

Inspectors will look for evidence that the space encourages independence, fosters learning, and reflects the needs and interests of the children. Highlighting children's involvement in shaping the environment—whether through their artwork, contributions to displays, or participation in setting up play areas—shows that the space is created with children in mind.

It's also important to ensure the environment reflects your setting's intent and philosophy. For example, if you emphasise outdoor learning, make sure your outdoor space showcases this, with clear links to how it supports the EYFS Statutory framework.

F is for Feedback

The Power of Constructive Feedback in Continuous Growth

Feedback is one of the most valuable tools in an early years setting.

It's not just about giving advice or praise - it's about fostering growth, building connections, and creating a culture where everyone feels heard, supported, and motivated. Feedback is a two-way street that touches every aspect of a setting: it nurtures children's confidence and learning, supports staff in their professional development, strengthens relationships with parents, and drives continuous improvement. When feedback is used thoughtfully, it becomes a cornerstone of a reflective and responsive environment that benefits everyone involved.

Feedback for Children: Nurturing Confidence and Growth

Feedback for children is about more than telling them they've done a "good job." It's about helping them understand what they're doing well, encouraging effort, and building resilience for when things don't go as planned.

Positive reinforcement is key.

Specific, meaningful feedback like, "I loved the way you tried lots of different pieces to finish that puzzle" helps children understand exactly what they did well. This kind of feedback is far more effective than generic praise, as it reinforces specific behaviours and skills. It's not just about the outcome; it's about recognising the process and effort behind it.

Fostering a growth mindset in children is equally important.

When we focus on effort and persistence, we teach them that learning is a journey, not a destination.

For example, saying, "You worked so hard to stack those blocks, even when they kept falling over. Well done for keeping at it!" helps children see challenges as opportunities to learn rather than barriers to success. This mindset is a powerful tool that builds resilience and confidence, qualities they'll carry with them far beyond the setting.

Feedback in early years settings isn't always verbal—it often happens through play and interaction. A smile, a nod, or engaging alongside a child in their chosen activity shows them that their efforts are noticed and valued. These subtle, non-verbal cues can be just as impactful as spoken words, especially for younger children who may still be developing their language skills.

Feedback for Staff: Creating a Culture of Professional Growth

Just as feedback supports children's development, it's essential for staff, too. Constructive feedback helps practitioners reflect on their practice, identify areas for improvement, and grow in their roles. The key is to strike a balance: celebrate successes while offering supportive guidance for development.

Feedback shouldn't be reserved for formal appraisals. Regular, informal check-ins create a continuous dialogue that keeps feedback flowing in a natural and supportive way. Whether it's a quick word of encouragement after a successful activity or a reflective chat about a challenging moment, these interactions show staff that their efforts are valued. Team meetings and peer observations also provide opportunities for shared learning and collaborative feedback, strengthening the team as a whole.

Peer-to-peer feedback is another powerful tool. Encouraging staff to observe and provide constructive feedback to one another fosters a culture of trust and mutual support. For example, one practitioner might share ideas for improving a storytime session or offer praise for how a colleague handled a tricky behaviour situation. When delivered professionally and respectfully, peer feedback builds confidence and strengthens practice across the team.

Feedback from Parents: Building Trust and Collaboration

Parents are an integral part of the early years community and their feedback is invaluable. Open and transparent communication helps build trust, ensuring that parents feel involved in their child's learning journey and confident in the care provided by the setting.

Regular opportunities for feedback are essential. Parent questionnaires, informal chats, or even a suggestion box can provide insights into what's working well and where improvements could be made. For example, a parent might suggest more outdoor play opportunities or share ideas for better communication about their child's day. Listening to and acting on these suggestions shows parents that their voices matter. It's not only children's voices we need to listen to.

Feedback should go both ways. Providing parents with constructive feedback about their child's progress helps them feel informed and empowered to support learning at home. For instance, sharing examples like, "We've noticed Ellie is showing an interest in numbers— perhaps you could count steps together at home" fosters collaboration and consistency between the setting and home.

Parent-practitioner meetings are another vital feedback tool. Preparing for these meetings with specific examples of the child's development ensures a meaningful and constructive conversation. At the same time, encouraging parents to share their observations and concerns creates a balanced, two-way exchange that benefits the child.

Feedback from Children: Hearing Their Voices

Children are at the heart of everything we do, so it's essential to involve them in the feedback process. Even the youngest children can express their preferences and opinions, helping shape the environment and activities to better suit their needs and interests.

Simple questions like, "What was your favourite part of today?" or "Is there something you'd like to play with tomorrow?" give children a voice in their learning journey. Their answers might surprise you and offer new ideas for planning activities or organising resources.

Non-verbal feedback from children is just as important. Observing how they engage with activities, toys, and routines provides valuable insights. For instance, if a group of children consistently avoids a particular area, it might indicate that the space or resources need adjusting. Paying attention to these cues ensures that the setting remains child-centred and responsive.

Feedback for Continuous Improvement: Reflection and Action

Feedback is only useful if it leads to meaningful change. Regularly reviewing and reflecting on feedback helps identify areas for improvement and turn them into actionable steps.

Reflection meetings with staff provide a dedicated space to discuss feedback and develop action plans. For example, if parents have suggested more communication about their child's day, the team might decide to introduce daily update sheets or a communication app.

Quality Improvement Plans (QIPs) are another effective way to formalise feedback-driven changes. Documenting goals, strategies, and progress not only keeps everyone focused but also shows parents and inspectors that feedback is taken seriously. Sharing these plans with families and staff fosters a sense of ownership and collaboration.

Handling Negative Feedback: Opportunities for Growth

Negative feedback isn't always easy to hear, but it's an opportunity to learn and grow. Whether it comes from parents, staff, or inspectors, the key is to approach it with an open mind and a willingness to improve.

Listening carefully to concerns and acknowledging their validity is the first step. For example, if a parent raises an issue about communication, responding with empathy - "Thank you for sharing that; we'll review how we can improve"—shows a commitment to resolving the problem. Following up with concrete actions, like scheduling a meeting or introducing a new system, demonstrates accountability and builds trust.

Using Feedback for Inspections: Demonstrating Reflective Practice

Feedback plays a crucial role in inspections, as it demonstrates reflective practice and a commitment to continuous improvement. Inspectors will want to see evidence of how feedback is gathered, reviewed, and acted upon.

Documenting feedback processes is essential. This might include parent surveys, staff appraisals, peer observation notes, or children's comments and preferences. Keeping records of how feedback has informed changes—like adjusting routines or introducing new resources—shows that your setting values input and uses it to enhance quality.

Self-evaluation tools (SEF) are another important tool. Including examples of feedback-driven improvements in your SEF demonstrates that your setting is proactive and responsive. For instance, noting that parent feedback led to the introduction of a sensory area highlights your commitment to meeting children's needs.

G is for Governance

Governance is all about how things are run, whether it's a business, a charity, or even a government. It's the systems, processes, and practices that make sure everything works smoothly, decisions are made wisely, and everyone involved is held accountable. In essence, it's the behind-the-scenes structure that keeps things ticking along, ensuring transparency and balancing the needs of everyone involved.

Strong Leadership for a High-Quality Setting

Governance in an early years setting is the foundation for creating a well-managed, high-quality environment that prioritises children's development and well-being. It encompasses the systems, structures and your leadership practices that ensure your setting runs smoothly, complies with regulations and continually strives for quality. With strong governance, settings are better equipped to navigate challenges, maintain high standards and build a thriving community of children, families and staff. At its core, governance is about accountability, strategic direction, and fostering an environment where everyone can succeed and thrive.

Clear Leadership and Vision

A strong early years setting is built on a clear vision and set of values that guide its daily operations and long-term goals. These principles provide a shared sense of purpose for everyone involved, from management to staff and families.

For example, a vision of "nurturing confident, curious learners in a caring and inclusive environment" can serve as a guide for all decisions, from curriculum planning to the design of the physical space.

Leadership is a critical element of governance, ensuring that this vision is communicated effectively and reflected in practice. A well-governed setting relies on leaders who are approachable, decisive and able to inspire their team. Strong leadership sets the tone for the entire setting, promoting a culture of collaboration, respect, and continuous improvement.

Clear roles and responsibilities are another hallmark of good governance. When everyone understands their role—whether it's the manager overseeing operations, the room leader planning learning activities, or the support staff ensuring the setting runs smoothly—the entire team functions more effectively. Role clarity not only streamlines daily operations but also prevents misunderstandings and duplication of effort, creating a more harmonious working environment.

Accountability and Compliance

Governance is the backbone of accountability in any early years setting. It ensures that all practices are aligned with national regulations and frameworks, such as the Early Years Foundation Stage (EYFS) in the UK. Compliance with these standards isn't just about avoiding welfare actions—it's about ensuring the highest quality of care and education for children.

Policies and procedures play a central role in achieving compliance. A well-governed setting will have clear, up-to-date policies covering safeguarding, health and safety, equal opportunities, and more. These documents aren't just for inspections—they're living tools that guide everyday practice and provide a framework for decision-making. For example, a safeguarding policy should outline how concerns are reported, while a health and safety policy ensures that risks are regularly assessed and mitigated.

Financial accountability is another key aspect of governance. Managing a setting's budget effectively ensures that resources are allocated where they're needed most—whether it's investing in staff training, purchasing new equipment, or maintaining the physical environment. Regular financial audits and transparent reporting build trust among stakeholders, including parents and funding bodies. Sound financial management is essential for sustaining a setting that is both high-quality and financially stable.

Continuous Improvement

Strong governance isn't just about maintaining the status quo; it's about fostering a culture of continuous improvement. This begins with regular self-evaluation and reflective practice. Governance structures should support the leadership team and staff in assessing what's working well and identifying areas for growth. Tools like self-evaluation forms (SEFs) and quality improvement plans (QIPs) provide a structured way to track progress and set actionable goals.

For example, a self-evaluation might reveal that while the setting excels in promoting children's language development, there's room to improve outdoor learning opportunities. Governance ensures that these insights are translated into meaningful action, such as investing in new outdoor equipment or providing training on outdoor pedagogy.

Staff development is another critical focus. Effective governance prioritises ongoing professional development, recognising that a skilled and motivated workforce is essential for delivering high-quality care and education. Whether it's through regular training sessions, mentoring, or access to external qualifications, investing in staff benefits the entire setting. A commitment to staff development not only raises the standard of practice but also boosts morale and retention, creating a positive working environment where everyone feels valued.

Governance and Inspection

Inspections are a key moment when governance comes under scrutiny. Inspectors will want to see clear evidence of leadership, accountability, and strategic planning. A well-governed setting will have robust safeguarding procedures, up-to-date policies, and a clear vision for continuous improvement—all of which demonstrate a commitment to achieving the best outcomes for children.

Documentation is crucial during inspections. Governance structures should be clearly outlined, with records showing how decisions are made and implemented. For example, meeting minutes might detail discussions on resource allocation, while action plans could highlight steps taken to address areas identified for improvement. Inspectors are particularly interested in how governance supports reflective practice, so be prepared to show how feedback from staff, parents, and children is used to drive change.

Strategic planning is another area of focus. A strong governance framework will include a clear strategic plan that outlines the setting's goals and priorities. This might include enhancing the curriculum, improving accessibility, or increasing parental engagement. Inspectors value evidence that the setting is proactive and forward-thinking, with governance structures that support long-term success.

Fostering Collaboration and Trust

Effective governance isn't just about policies and procedures—it's about building strong relationships and fostering a sense of trust among all stakeholders. Parents, staff, and external partners all play a role in shaping the success of a setting, and governance should provide opportunities for collaboration and input.

For parents, governance might involve regular communication about the setting's goals, policies, and achievements. This could be through newsletters, parent forums, or open days where families can see how decisions are made and how their feedback is incorporated. Transparent communication builds trust and helps parents feel invested in the setting's success.

For staff, governance means creating a supportive environment where their voices are heard. Regular team meetings, open-door policies, and opportunities for professional growth ensure that staff feel valued and empowered. A well-governed setting encourages collaboration, with leaders and practitioners working together to solve challenges and celebrate successes.

External partnerships are another important aspect of governance. Whether it's working with local schools, community organisations, or regulatory bodies, strong governance ensures that these relationships are managed effectively. Collaboration with external partners can enhance the setting's resources, support transitions for children, and provide access to valuable expertise.

Overcoming Challenges Through Governance

Every setting faces challenges, whether it's managing funding constraints, addressing staff turnover, or meeting the needs of a diverse community. Strong governance provides the tools and structures to navigate these challenges effectively.

For example, if an early years setting is facing financial difficulties, governance might involve reviewing the budget, seeking alternative funding sources, or implementing cost-saving measures. Similarly, if staff retention is an issue, governance could focus on enhancing professional development opportunities or improving working conditions to boost morale.

Governance also plays a key role in addressing external challenges, such as changes to regulatory requirements or shifts in community demographics. By staying informed and adaptable, a well-governed setting can respond proactively to these changes, ensuring that it continues to meet the needs of children and families.

The Impact of Strong Governance

When governance is done well, its impact is felt across every aspect of the setting.

Children benefit from a stable, well-resourced environment where their needs are prioritised. Staff feel supported, motivated, and equipped to deliver high-quality care and education. Families trust that their children are in safe hands, and inspectors see a setting that is organised, reflective, and committed to excellence.

Governance might not be the most visible part of an early years setting, but it is undoubtedly one of the most important. It provides the structure and accountability needed to ensure that every decision is made with the best interests of children, staff, and families at heart.

H is for Health and Safety

Creating a Safe and Secure Environment for Children

In any early years setting, health and safety form the backbone of daily operations. These foundational principles ensure children are nurtured in an environment where they can learn, explore, and play without unnecessary risks. Beyond fulfilling legal obligations, a robust health and safety policy signals a commitment to creating a safe, supportive space for children and staff alike. For children, this means a secure environment where they feel confident to try new things. For parents, it provides peace of mind, knowing that their children's well-being is the top priority.

Health and safety aren't just about preventing harm—they're about enabling growth and discovery in a controlled environment. A proactive approach fosters a culture of care, where staff are vigilant, prepared and united in their mission to protect the most vulnerable members of society. This attention to detail reassures parents and contributes to the overall reputation of the setting, ensuring trust and long-term success.

Daily Safety Practices

The daily rhythm of a day nursery, preschool or childminding setting should prioritise safety, embedding vigilance into every activity. Regular risk assessments form the foundation of this practice, ensuring hazards are identified and managed promptly. These assessments might involve checking outdoor equipment for damage, ensuring small toys are not choking hazards, and reviewing the overall layout to minimise risks during active play.

Importantly, risk assessments should not be treated as paperwork to file away but as a tool that actively shape the environment.

Childproofing measures are essential in creating a safe space. From covers to outdoor sand trays and secure gates to proper storage for cleaning products, each precaution reduces the chance of accidents. Equipment and furniture should be age-appropriate, sturdy, and frequently inspected for wear and tear. When children feel safe, they are more likely to engage in meaningful play and exploration, which are crucial for their development.

Equally critical is first aid readiness. Ideally all staff should be trained in paediatric first aid, with regular refresher courses to keep their skills sharp. First aid kits must be fully stocked and easily accessible at all times. Knowing how to respond confidently to injuries—whether minor or serious—can make a world of difference. A swift and professional response reassures parents and creates an atmosphere of trust among staff and children.

Hygiene and Cleanliness

Maintaining a clean environment is a cornerstone of health and safety. It's not just about appearances—hygiene directly impacts the health of everyone in the setting. Teaching children the importance of handwashing is an excellent starting point. Staff can make this routine engaging by introducing songs, visual prompts, or games that encourage thorough washing. These habits not only reduce the spread of germs but also instil lifelong practices in children.

A comprehensive cleaning schedule ensures high-touch surfaces like tables, toys, and door handles are disinfected daily. During peak illness seasons, such as winter, these efforts should be intensified. Soft furnishings and dress-up clothes also require regular cleaning to minimise the spread of germs. When was the last time your dressing up clothes had a wash? Consistency in cleaning routines protects everyone, from children with developing immune systems to staff who are exposed daily.

Food hygiene is another key consideration, especially in settings that provide meals or snacks. Staff should receive food hygiene training to ensure preparation areas meet strict standards. All staff who are responsible for preparing and handling food must receive training in food hygiene. Allergies and dietary requirements must be carefully managed, with clear communication among staff to prevent mix-ups. Transparency about food practices builds trust with parents, reinforcing the setting's commitment to health and safety.

Emergency Preparedness

While emergencies may be rare, being prepared for them is non-negotiable. Regular fire drills ensure both children and staff know what to do in case of evacuation. Fire exits must remain clear and well-marked, and alarms and extinguishers should be tested frequently. By practising calmly and routinely, children become familiar with these procedures without unnecessary fear, embedding a sense of preparedness.

Accidents, while unfortunate, should be handled with professionalism and care. Detailed records of every incident—however minor—are essential. These logs not only ensure accountability but also help identify recurring issues that may require adjustments, such as modifying the environment or adding extra supervision in certain areas. This does mean the forms needs to signed and dated.

Preparedness extends beyond physical safety. Staff should be equipped to handle medical emergencies, including allergic reactions or seizures, with confidence. Tailored action plans for children with specific medical needs ensure swift and appropriate responses, further contributing to a secure environment.

Promoting Well-Being

Health and safety go hand in hand with emotional well-being. A truly safe environment is one where children feel valued, heard, and supported. Emotional security plays a crucial role in a child's overall development. Simple gestures, like comforting a child when they're upset or providing a quiet corner for children who feel overwhelmed, make a significant difference in their sense of safety.

Teaching safe behaviours is another way to promote well-being. For instance, showing children how to handle scissors or navigate the space safely lays the groundwork for lifelong habits. Staff should use positive reinforcement and language. For example, phrases like "Let's walk indoors to stay safe" are more constructive than simply saying "Don't run." This approach builds trust and helps children internalise the value of safe choices.

Health and Safety and Inspections

During inspections, health and safety practices often come under close scrutiny. Inspectors expect to see robust policies and evidence of their implementation. This includes up-to-date risk assessments, well-maintained accident logs and staff training records, particularly for first aid. Being organised and prepared for inspections not only demonstrates compliance but also highlights the setting's commitment to excellence.

Health and safety practices should be visible in everyday interactions. Inspectors will observe how staff supervise children during play, transition between activities, and respond to potential hazards. Embedding health and safety into the culture of the setting ensures that these practices are more than just policies—they are integral to the way the setting operates. A strong health and safety culture ultimately benefits everyone, from children and parents to staff and stakeholders.

The Importance of Communication

Effective communication is the glue that holds health and safety practices together. Staff must be well-informed and aligned on procedures, whether it's responding to a fire alarm or managing daily cleaning tasks. Regular training and team meetings provide opportunities to refresh knowledge, address concerns, and reinforce the importance of shared responsibility.

Parents are key partners in maintaining a safe environment. Clear communication about policies—such as illness protocols or allergy management—fosters trust and cooperation. Sharing updates through newsletters, handbooks, or conversations during pick-up and drop-off ensures parents feel involved and informed. When parents understand and support the setting's approach to health and safety, it creates a collaborative environment that benefits everyone.

Adapting to Individual Needs

Every child is unique, and health and safety practices must reflect this. Tailored plans are essential for children with allergies, medical conditions, or additional needs. For instance, a child with a severe nut allergy might require a personalised emergency action plan, while a child with sensory sensitivities might need a quiet space to retreat during busy periods.

Collaboration with parents is vital when developing these plans. By involving them in the process, settings can ensure the child's specific needs are met while building trust and reassurance. Staff must also be fully briefed on these plans to respond appropriately in any situation. Adapting practices to individual needs not only ensures safety but also promotes inclusivity and equality.

Why Health and Safety Matter

Health and safety are more than just policies—they are the foundation of a nurturing, effective early years setting. A well-executed approach protects children, empowers staff, and reassures parents. By prioritising both physical and emotional safety, settings create an environment where children can flourish, staff can work confidently, and parents can trust in the care provided. The ripple effect of strong health and safety practices extends far beyond the immediate environment, contributing to a healthier, happier community.

I is for Inclusion and Accessibility

Creating an Inclusive Environment for All Children

Inclusion is the beating heart of high-quality early years education. It's about ensuring that every child, regardless of their background, abilities, or culture, feels valued, supported, and truly part of the setting. An inclusive approach doesn't just benefit individual children; it enriches the entire community, fostering empathy, respect and understanding among children, staff, and families. Inclusion is about removing barriers, celebrating differences, and ensuring that every child has the same opportunities to thrive.

Cultural and Social Inclusion

Creating an inclusive environment starts with recognising and celebrating diversity. Your setting should be a mirror of the rich variety of cultures, languages, and family structures in your community. This can be achieved by thoughtfully choosing books, toys, and displays that represent a wide range of backgrounds and experiences. For example, books featuring characters from diverse cultures or toys that reflect different abilities and family dynamics help children see themselves and others in the materials they interact with.

Celebrating festivals and traditions from various cultures is another way to foster inclusion. These celebrations not only introduce children to different ways of life but also create opportunities for families to share their own traditions and feel a sense of pride and belonging. Whether it's Diwali, Lunar New Year, or a local harvest festival, these moments bring everyone together in a spirit of mutual respect and curiosity.

Language can also be a bridge to inclusion. For children who speak multiple languages, providing bilingual books, visual aids, and opportunities to share their home language with peers can help them feel understood and valued. Encouraging staff to learn simple greetings or key phrases in the languages spoken by families in your setting can make a big difference, showing that you are committed to building a welcoming and connected environment.

Supporting Children with Special Educational Needs and Disabilities (SEND)

Inclusion means ensuring that every child, regardless of their abilities, has access to learning opportunities and feels fully part of the setting. For children with special educational needs and disabilities (SEND), this requires thoughtful planning, tailored support, and a commitment to meeting their unique needs.

Individual support plans are a crucial tool for supporting children with SEND. These plans should highlight each child's strengths, outline the challenges they face and specify the strategies used to support their learning and development. Involving parents and external professionals in creating and reviewing these plans ensures they remain relevant and effective.

Adaptive resources can make all the difference for children with physical, sensory, or cognitive needs. For example, visual timetables help children with communication difficulties understand the day's routine, while sensory toys or specialised seating can provide comfort and support. The aim is to create an environment where every child can engage fully, regardless of their abilities.

Collaboration with specialists, such as speech therapists, occupational therapists, or SENCOs, is key to providing effective support. These professionals bring expertise and insights that help settings tailor their approaches to meet each child's needs. Regular communication and a team approach ensure that children receive consistent, targeted support that helps them reach their full potential.

Promoting Social Inclusion

Social inclusion is about creating an environment where all children can play, learn, and grow together. Inclusive play is a powerful way to break down barriers and build connections between children of different abilities and backgrounds. By designing activities that cater to a range of learning styles and abilities, you create opportunities for all children to participate and succeed.

For example, group activities like collaborative art projects or sensory play sessions encourage interaction and cooperation, helping children build friendships and develop social skills.

Teaching kindness, empathy, and respect is another essential element of social inclusion. Stories, discussions, and role-modelling can help children understand and appreciate differences. For instance, reading books about characters who overcome challenges or talking about how to include someone who might feel left out fosters a culture of acceptance. When children learn that everyone has unique strengths and needs, they develop the empathy and understanding that will serve them well throughout their lives.

Parent and Family Involvement

An inclusive setting doesn't just focus on children—it extends to families as well. Engaging with parents in a way that respects their individual needs, backgrounds, and preferences is vital. This might mean providing information in different languages or formats, such as translated newsletters or visual guides. Being sensitive to cultural or social factors that may affect a family's engagement helps create an environment where everyone feels welcome.

Partnership with parents is especially important for children with additional needs. Parents are experts on their own children, and their insights are invaluable in shaping the support provided by the setting. Regular communication, whether through face-to-face meetings, daily updates, or shared support plans, ensures that parents feel heard and involved. Collaborative decision-making empowers parents and reinforces the message that their contributions are valued.

Inclusion and Inspections

During inspections, inclusion will be under the spotlight. Inspectors want to see evidence that your setting actively promotes inclusion and ensures equal access for all children. This might include documentation of how you support children with SEND, adapt activities, and celebrate diversity.

Your policies and practices should clearly reflect an inclusive ethos. For example, risk assessments that consider the needs of children with mobility challenges or planning documents that show how activities are differentiated demonstrate that inclusion is embedded in your practice. Inspectors will also look for evidence of staff training in areas such as SEND or cultural competency, as this shows a commitment to ongoing learning and improvement.

Embedding Inclusion into Daily Practice

Inclusion isn't just about policies or plans—it's about the day-to-day actions that make children and families feel seen, respected have a sense of belonging and feel valued. This might mean adapting a popular group activity to ensure a child with sensory sensitivities can participate or making space in a busy schedule for a quiet moment with a child who needs extra reassurance.

The physical environment plays a role too. An inclusive setting has spaces and resources that cater to a wide range of needs. Quiet corners, sensory-friendly areas and accessible equipment ensure that every child can engage in their own way. Displays that celebrate children's work, cultures and achievements further reinforce the message that everyone belongs.

Overcoming Challenges to Inclusion

Creating an inclusive setting isn't always easy—it requires flexibility, creativity, and a willingness to learn. Challenges like limited resources or competing priorities can make it difficult to meet every need, but a proactive approach can help. For example, partnerships with local charities or community organisations can provide access to additional resources or expertise.

It's also important to address unconscious bias or assumptions that may affect how inclusion is implemented. Reflective practice, open conversations and ongoing training can help staff recognise and challenge these biases, ensuring that every decision is made with the best interests of all children in mind.

The Impact of Inclusion

When inclusion is at the heart of a setting, the impact is profound. Children develop a strong sense of belonging and confidence, knowing that their unique strengths and experiences are valued. They learn to see differences as opportunities for connection and growth, rather than barriers.

Staff, too, benefit from working in an inclusive environment. They develop a deeper understanding of diversity and gain the skills to support children with a wide range of needs. Families feel reassured and empowered, knowing their children are cared for in a setting that celebrates individuality and fosters community.

Understanding Accessibility

Accessibility in an Early Years setting is about creating a space where every single child and practitioner feels like they belong, can join in and has the chance to shine.

Yes, you have heard it from me again. That shine word.

It's not just about meeting legal requirements or ticking off a checklist; it's about rolling up your sleeves and thinking,

"What can we do to make sure every child and practitioner feels valued and included here?"

When was the last time you said that!

Barriers come in all shapes and sizes—physical, sensory, cognitive, or emotional—and it's our job to tackle them with creativity and care. Sometimes it's as simple as rearranging a few chairs to make way for a wheelchair.

Other times, it's about introducing visual aids to help a child better understand their day and feel more secure. The key is recognising that every child is so unique—what makes one child feel supported might not work for another. It's about rolling up our sleeves, thinking outside the box, and making sure every child can fully take part and feel included.

It's not about one-size-fits-all results.

For example, if a child struggles with loud environments, creating a quiet, cosy corner can make a huge difference. Or, if transitions feel overwhelming, which we know with the number of audits we complete that using visual aids and timetable or a favourite comfort item can help smooth the process. Accessibility isn't just about the big things; it's often the small, thoughtful adjustments that help a child feel safe and included.

Physical Accessibility

Let's start with the basics as this is the best way to start and sometimes we just need to start back at the beginning again.

We need to be making sure our setting is easy to get around. If you've got a child in a wheelchair or one with mobility challenges, having ramps, wide doorways, and enough space to move freely is essential. Have you ever looked at it through the eyes of a child. If not, please take the time to do that. It really helps. Even simple things like not cluttering up paths can make life easier for everyone, including us as practitioners.

Toilet Facilities

Accessible toilet facilities aren't just a nice-to-have—they're a MUST. Grab rails, lower sinks, and enough space for a practitioner to help if needed are game-changers. These adjustments help children maintain their dignity and independence. Also think about how cluttered the toilets are. We see this time and again where everything is stored in the toilet area and causes so much stress for little ones.

Outdoor Spaces

Outdoor play is for everyone, FACT. Think about sensory paths, equipment that works for all abilities, and surfaces that are safe and easy to navigate. Think about when you risk assess these areas... and yes, it is that dreaded word that seems to come out of my mouth quite frequently. This might mean adding a sandpit that's raised or a balancing beam with extra support.

Every child should be able to enjoy the outdoors, no matter their needs.

Sensory Accessibility

For children with visual impairments, high-contrast colours on signs and resources can make all the difference. Think about adding tactile indicators on handrails and steps too. And don't forget resources like large-print books or materials in Braille—they're brilliant for helping children access learning and a good way of showing cultural capital! This is where we need to reflect on the colours that we use. We know that the colour beige is often used in settings and this book is not the place for my opinions. But doing some research on what I wanted to include in this book actually got me thinking about colours and the impact this has on children including those with additional needs.

Hearing Accessibility

For children with hearing impairments, your setting's noise level is crucial. Reducing background noise (we all know how chaotic early years settings can get!) and using visual aids like picture cards or basic sign language can really help. If you can, look into assistive tools like hearing loops—it might be a bigger investment, but the impact can be huge. Especially if you have children who are hearing impaired.

Sensory-Friendly Spaces

Let's face it, sometimes we all need a bit of calm in an early years setting—and for some children, it's absolutely essential. A thoughtfully designed sensory-friendly space can be a haven, offering a moment of peace when the hustle and bustle becomes too much. And don't we all need that sometimes.

Soft lighting, textures and neutral colours create an environment that feels safe and calming, allowing children to decompress and find their balance.

It's not just about providing a retreat; it's about recognising when a child needs time to regulate their emotions or sensory input. These spaces are NOT a "time out", they're a "time to reset," giving children the chance to recharge so they can rejoin the group when they're ready, feeling calmer, more confident and in control.

Cognitive and Developmental Accessibility

In an early years setting, every child learns at their own pace and in their own way, so it's vital to have a variety of teaching and learning materials that cater to different developmental stages and abilities. Think of it as meeting children where they are, rather than expecting them to fit into one standard approach.

Visual timetables, again are a great tool for helping children understand the structure of their day, especially those who find transitions challenging or need a bit more predictability to feel secure. They break the day into manageable chunks and allow children to see what's coming next, giving them a sense of control and reducing anxiety.

Simple instructions, broken down step by step, make tasks more accessible for children who might struggle with verbal or complex directions. Pairing spoken instructions with visual cues or gestures can help reinforce understanding, ensuring no child feels left behind.

Hands-on activities are another brilliant way to support cognitive and developmental accessibility. These activities allow children to explore concepts through play and experimentation, appealing to their natural curiosity.

From sensory bins to puzzles, tactile learning provides a concrete way for children to grasp abstract ideas. For example, counting objects or sorting colours can be far more engaging and effective than trying to explain numbers or patterns through words alone.

It's also important to consider inclusive resources that reflect the diverse abilities and interests of your children. Adaptive tools, like chunky crayons and chalks for children who have difficulty with fine motor skills, or auditory resources like Talking tins for children who respond well to sounds, can open learning for children who may otherwise struggle with traditional methods.

By creating a rich, varied, and inclusive learning environment, you're not only making the day more accessible but also showing children that their individual needs are understood and valued. This approach builds confidence, fosters independence, and ensures that every child has the opportunity to engage, explore, and thrive.

Adaptable Activities

In an early years setting, adaptability is your best friend. Activities are never one-size-fits-all, and being ready to tweak them ensures that every child, regardless of their abilities, can take part and feel included. Sometimes it's as simple as breaking a task down into smaller, more manageable steps, giving children a clearer path to success. For instance, instead of asking a group of children to create a collage, you might first encourage one child to choose and stick one piece at a time, celebrating their progress along the way.

Other times, it's about providing a little extra support during group activities. This could mean assigning a buddy offering a visual demonstration or simply being nearby to lend a helping hand or a word of encouragement.

And we all need that, don't we?

These adjustments aren't about lowering expectations—they're about opening doors and showing children that their contributions are valued, no matter how big or small.

Adapting activities is more than just practical; it's a way of saying to every child, "You belong here, just as you are." When children see that their individual needs are met, they gain confidence, feel supported, and are more likely to engage actively and enthusiastically.

Inclusive Curriculum

Representation matters and in early years, it can make a world of difference. An inclusive curriculum is one that reflects the rich diversity of the children in your care—including those with disabilities—and shows them that their experiences and identities are valued.

Start with your books. Choose stories that feature characters with different abilities, backgrounds, and family structures. Picture books with diverse characters help children see themselves in the narratives and learn about others who might have different experiences.

Toys and resources also play a big role. Include dolls with hearing aids, wheelchairs, or limb differences, and puzzles or games that represent a variety of cultural traditions. These items might seem small, but they send a big message: "Everyone has a place here."

Beyond materials, think about how your curriculum celebrates inclusion. Use group discussions, circle times, and activities to talk about differences in a positive, age-appropriate way. For example, you might explore how everyone learns differently or invite children to share what makes them unique.

An inclusive curriculum doesn't just benefit children with diverse needs—it benefits all children. It fosters empathy, builds awareness, and creates a community where kindness and acceptance are the norm. It's about ensuring that every child feels seen, valued, and celebrated, not just as part of the group but for the individual they are.

Emotional and Social Accessibility

Building an emotionally inclusive environment is just as important as the physical side. It starts with staff who are trained to understand and respond to children's emotions and needs. Whether it's offering a cuddle remembering to ask if a child would like this first, a listening ear, or a quiet space, we need to show children that their feelings are valid. This is so important.

Encouraging children to work and play together is key to fostering an inclusive environment. Activities like cooperative games can help children build friendships and learn about kindness and empathy. Use group time to celebrate differences and teach children that it's okay to be unique—it's what makes us all special.

Staff Training and Awareness

Accessibility doesn't happen by accident. Staff need regular training to understand how to support children with different needs, from using adaptive equipment to managing sensory sensitivities. This isn't about turning everyone into experts—it's about building confidence and awareness.

Collaboration with Specialists

Don't forget to reach out to the professionals. Occupational therapists, speech and language therapists, and Area special educational needs coordinators (SENCOs) can offer valuable insights and strategies to help you make your setting more inclusive.

Parent and Family Engagement

Parents know their children best, so make sure you're talking to them regularly. Ask about their child's needs, what works at home, and any concerns they have. A good partnership with parents can make all the difference.

Families are an essential part of the puzzle when it comes to supporting children in early years settings, and sometimes, they need a bit of support themselves. Pointing families towards relevant resources and support groups can make a world of difference, especially for those navigating the challenges of raising a child with additional needs.

For many parents and carers, just knowing they're not alone can be a huge relief. It's not about giving them all the answers—it's about connecting them with people and organisations that can offer guidance, share experiences, and provide reassurance. Whether it's a local parent group, a national charity, or online forums, these networks can become a lifeline, offering practical advice and emotional support.

Encouraging families to access these resources also builds a sense of community. When parents meet others in similar situations, they can exchange ideas, celebrate milestones together, and lean on each other during tough times. This kind of peer support is often as valuable as professional advice, if not more so.

As early years practitioners, we're in a unique position to bridge that gap. Sharing information about support networks, advocacy groups, or workshops tailored to specific needs shows families that we're not just here for their children—we're here for them too. It's about fostering partnerships and letting parents know they're part of a team working together to give their child the best possible start.

Legal and Regulatory Compliance

Laws like the Equality Act 2010 aren't just hoops to jump through—they're there to make sure no child is left out. Make sure you're on top of what's required and always aim to go above and beyond.

Regular Audits

Checking in regularly on your accessibility provisions is a great way to spot areas for improvement. It's not about pointing fingers; it's about making your setting better for everyone.

When you prioritise accessibility, you create a space where every child feels welcome, supported and able to thrive. It's about seeing the child first, not their challenges, and showing them—and their families—that they matter. With a bit of planning, some creative thinking, and a lot of heart, you can make your setting a place where all children can flourish.

J is for Judgements

Understanding Ofsted's Focus and the Shift Away from Single-Word Judgements

In recent years, the way Ofsted evaluates early years settings has evolved significantly. One of the most anticipated changes is the move away from single-word judgements, which has been a long-debated aspect of inspections. This is due at the time of print from Sept 2025, but there has been not confirmation yet. This shift reflects a broader aim to provide more nuanced, meaningful feedback that truly supports continuous improvement rather than simply categorising settings into broad labels.

This change has significant implications for early years practitioners, managers and leaders. By understanding the key areas Ofsted focuses on, as well as the reasoning behind the move away from single-word judgements, you can better prepare for inspections and use the process as a tool for growth and reflection.

What Are Ofsted Judgements?

Ofsted inspections assess early years settings across several key areas to evaluate the quality of care and education provided. Traditionally, these judgements were summarised in single words: "Outstanding", "Good", "Requires Improvement", or "Inadequate". While these labels provided a snapshot of overall performance, they often oversimplified the complexities of running an early years setting and didn't always reflect the nuances of the work being done.

Inspectors' judgements are based on detailed criteria outlined in Ofsted's Education Inspection Framework (EIF). The framework focuses on four main areas, or "key judgements," which are:

1. Quality of Education

2. Behaviour and Attitudes

3. Personal Development

4. Leadership and Management

Each of these areas contributes to the overall judgement of the setting.

Why Is This Change Happening?

Single-word judgements often failed to capture the full picture of a setting's performance. For example, a "Good" judgement might overlook significant areas of excellence, while a "Requires Improvement" judgement could mask the progress a setting has made in specific areas.

Encouraging Growth: By moving away from labels, Ofsted aims to foster a more supportive approach to inspections, where the focus is on identifying actionable steps for improvement rather than assigning a label that may feel discouraging.

Reducing Pressure: Single-word judgements often created undue pressure on settings to achieve a specific grade, sometimes at the expense of focusing on genuine improvement. This change is intended to shift the emphasis to meaningful development.

The Key Areas of Judgement: A Closer Look

Let's explore the four main areas that Ofsted focuses on during inspections, with insights into how settings can prepare and demonstrate excellence.

Quality of Education

This is the heart of the inspection process, focusing on the intent, implementation, and impact of your curriculum. Inspectors look at how well the curriculum is designed to meet the needs of all children, how effectively it's delivered, and the outcomes it achieves.

Intent: What do you want children to learn? Your curriculum should have clear goals, be ambitious, and reflect the needs of the children in your care. For example, if many children in your setting come from multilingual homes, your curriculum might prioritise developing strong language and communication skills.

Implementation: How do you deliver the curriculum? Inspectors will observe how practitioners interact with children, adapt activities to their interests, and ensure all children are engaged and supported. For example, a practitioner might use storytelling, role-play, and group discussions to build communication skills in a way that's playful and accessible.

Impact: What are the outcomes for children? Inspectors will assess how well children are progressing, both in their development and their readiness for the next stage of learning. Evidence of impact might include children demonstrating curiosity, resilience, and independence in their play and learning.

Behaviour and Attitudes

This judgement focuses on how well your setting supports positive behaviour, emotional security, and attitudes to learning. Inspectors will look at how practitioners create a calm, respectful environment where children feel safe and valued.

Promoting Positive Behaviour: Practitioners should model and reinforce positive behaviours, such as sharing, turn-taking, and kindness. For example, using gentle reminders and praise to encourage cooperation during group activities.

Building Emotional Security: Inspectors will want to see how your setting supports children's emotional well-being. This might include having consistent key workers, creating cosy spaces for quiet time, and using resources like feelings charts to help children express their emotions.

Encouraging a Love of Learning:Children who are enthusiastic about exploring and trying new things demonstrate a positive attitude to learning. Practitioners can foster this by offering engaging, child-led activities that spark curiosity and excitement.

Personal Development

This area focuses on how well your setting supports children's overall development, including their physical health, emotional resilience, and understanding of the world.

Promoting Healthy Lifestyles: Inspectors will look at how you encourage physical activity, healthy eating, and self-care. For example, providing daily opportunities for outdoor play, offering nutritious snacks, and teaching children how to wash their hands properly.

Fostering Social Skills: Personal development also includes helping children build relationships, resolve conflicts, and develop empathy. Practitioners might use role-play, collaborative games, and discussions to promote these skills.

Celebrating Diversity: Inspectors will want to see how your setting reflects and respects the diverse backgrounds of the children in your care. This might include using multicultural resources, celebrating different festivals, and encouraging children to share their own experiences.

Leadership and Management

Strong leadership is essential for maintaining high standards across your setting. Inspectors will evaluate how well leaders support their team, ensure compliance with regulations, and create a culture of continuous improvement.

Supporting Staff: Effective leaders invest in their team's professional development, providing regular training, feedback, and opportunities for growth. For example, organising workshops on safeguarding or encouraging practitioners to pursue further qualifications.

Ensuring Compliance: Inspectors will check that policies and procedures are up-to-date, well-implemented, and understood by all staff. This includes areas like safeguarding, health and safety, and data protection.

Fostering a Positive Culture: A strong leadership team creates a setting where everyone feels valued, supported, and motivated to deliver their best. This might involve recognising staff achievements, promoting well-being, and encouraging reflective practice.

Preparing for the New Approach

As Ofsted moves away from single-word judgements, it's more important than ever to focus on the specifics of your practice. Here's how to prepare:

Know Your Strengths: Reflect on what your setting does well and be ready to share examples with inspectors. This could include innovative activities, strong partnerships with parents, or successful interventions for children with additional needs.

Address Areas for Improvement: Use self-evaluation and feedback to identify areas that need attention. Create action plans to address these gaps and track your progress.

Empower Your Team:Ensure that all staff understand the key areas of judgement and feel confident discussing their role in achieving them. Regular training and reflective discussions can help build this confidence.

Engage Families: Strong partnerships with parents and carers demonstrate your commitment to collaboration and transparency. Share updates on children's progress, involve families in activities, and invite their feedback.

Judgements are an integral part of the inspection process, but they're more than just a grade or label. They're a tool for reflection, a framework for growth, and a chance to celebrate the incredible work happening in early years settings every day. By understanding the key areas of focus and embracing the shift toward more nuanced feedback, you can approach inspections with confidence, knowing that your setting is delivering the very best for the children in your care.

K is for Knowledge

Ensuring Staff Are Well-Informed and Skilled

The heartbeat of any successful early years setting is its people. Knowledge is what transforms good practice into outstanding outcomes for children. It's not just about qualifications on paper—it's about staying informed, adaptable and committed to learning. When staff are equipped with deep, up-to-date knowledge, children thrive, parents trust, and the setting as a whole flourishes.

Knowledge isn't static. The world of early years education is ever-evolving, with new research, approaches, and regulations shaping how we support young children. That's why fostering a culture of ongoing learning and professional curiosity is essential.

Understanding Child Development

The foundation of every practitioner's role is a thorough understanding of child development. This knowledge allows staff to recognise and respond to the developmental milestones that mark a child's growth across physical, cognitive, social, and emotional domains. It's about knowing when to celebrate achievements like a child's first independent steps or their growing ability to share, and when to step in with additional support if something doesn't seem quite right.

The Early Years Foundation Stage (EYFS) framework provides the backbone of this knowledge in the UK. Staff must be confident in applying the EYFS principles to their daily practice, ensuring that their planning, observations, and interactions are developmentally appropriate. For example, understanding the importance of play in cognitive development might lead a practitioner to encourage imaginative role-play to help a child develop problem-solving skills.

But development isn't a one-size-fits-all journey. Knowledgeable staff understand that every child develops at their own pace and in their own way. Differentiating activities to match individual needs and interests is key. For instance, while one child may be captivated by physical activities like jumping or climbing, another might prefer quiet, focused tasks like puzzles or drawing. Recognising and embracing these differences ensures that all children feel supported and engaged.

Continuous Professional Development

Knowledge doesn't stop growing the day someone earns their qualification. In fact, that's just the starting point. Early years practitioners must stay up-to-date with the latest research, methodologies, and regulatory requirements to provide the best possible care and education.

Ongoing training is essential. Topics such as safeguarding, special educational needs and disabilities (SEND), mental health, and new pedagogical approaches are just a few of the areas where regular professional development can make a huge difference. For example, attending a course on trauma-informed practice might help a practitioner better understand and support a child who has experienced adverse experiences.

A culture of learning benefits the entire team. Staff should be encouraged to share insights and strategies with each other after attending training or workshops. Regular team meetings, peer observations, and collaborative discussions can create a dynamic environment where everyone learns from one another. For example, a staff member who has learned about outdoor learning might lead a session on how to integrate nature-based activities into the curriculum.

Specialist Knowledge

Certain areas of knowledge require a deeper understanding, particularly when it comes to supporting children with additional needs or ensuring their safety.

Supporting Children with SEND

Children with special educational needs and disabilities (SEND) deserve the same opportunities to thrive as their peers, and it's the responsibility of the setting to make this happen. This requires staff to have specific knowledge about a range of needs, from sensory processing issues to behavioural challenges.

For example, a child with autism might benefit from a visual timetable to help them navigate transitions during the day. Staff must know how to adapt the environment, activities, and their own interactions to create a supportive and inclusive space. Building strong relationships with external professionals, such as occupational therapists or speech therapists, ensures that children receive tailored support that addresses their unique needs.

Safeguarding Expertise

Safeguarding is an area of knowledge that simply cannot be overlooked. Every member of staff must know how to identify signs of abuse, neglect, or other safeguarding concerns, as well as the procedures for reporting them. This knowledge isn't just about ticking a box—it's about protecting children and ensuring their welfare.

Regular safeguarding training ensures that staff are confident in their responsibilities and prepared to act if a concern arises. For example, understanding the importance of listening to children and recognising behavioural changes can help practitioners identify and respond to potential issues early.

Knowledge and Inspections

During inspections, the expertise of your team will be under the spotlight. Inspectors want to see that staff have the knowledge required to support children's learning and development effectively.

This means staff need to be able to articulate their understanding of key concepts in early childhood education, such as how play supports learning or how to plan for children with varying needs. For example, if an inspector asks about how a child with speech delay is supported, a knowledgeable practitioner might explain how they use visual aids and simplified language to encourage communication.

Evidence of continuous professional development also demonstrates a commitment to maintaining high standards. Training logs, certificates and records of in-house workshops can provide clear proof that the team is staying current and informed.

Embedding Knowledge into Practice

Having knowledge is one thing, but applying it effectively is what truly makes a difference. Practitioners must be able to translate what they know into meaningful actions that benefit children.

For example, understanding the role of emotional well-being in learning might lead to the creation of a quiet corner where children can self-regulate when they're feeling overwhelmed. Similarly, knowledge of child-led approaches could inspire practitioners to follow a child's interest in transport by setting up a role-play bus station or introducing books about vehicles.

The environment itself can reflect the team's knowledge. A well-thought-out space that promotes independence, creativity, and exploration shows that staff understand the principles of high-quality early years education. Displays that showcase children's work and achievements further demonstrate this knowledge in action.

The Role of Leadership in Building Knowledge

Strong leadership plays a vital role in fostering a knowledgeable team. Leaders and managers should prioritise training and development, ensuring that all staff have access to the resources and opportunities they need to grow.

Mentoring and coaching are powerful tools for sharing knowledge within the team. More experienced staff can guide newer practitioners, offering insights and advice based on years of practice. This not only builds confidence but also creates a sense of shared purpose and collaboration.

Overcoming Barriers to Professional Growth

Sometimes, settings face challenges in keeping their teams up-to-date with training and development. Limited budgets or time constraints can make it difficult to prioritise professional growth. However, there are creative solutions to these challenges.

For example, online training courses often offer affordable and flexible options for staff development. But please remember the impact of these courses. What do you get from them? Partnering with local authorities or early years networks can also provide access to free or subsidised training opportunities.

Encouraging staff to take ownership of their learning is another way to overcome barriers. Providing access to books, journals, or online resources allows practitioners to explore topics of interest independently.

The Impact of Knowledge

When staff are knowledgeable, the benefits ripple throughout the entire setting. Children receive high-quality care and education tailored to their needs, fostering their development and well-being. Parents feel reassured, knowing their children are supported by skilled professionals. Staff themselves experience greater job satisfaction and confidence, contributing to a positive and motivated team culture.

Knowledge also builds resilience. A team that understands the principles of child development, safeguarding, and inclusive practice is better equipped to handle challenges, whether it's supporting a child through a difficult transition or navigating changes in regulations.

L is for Learning and Development

Supporting Holistic Growth Through Engaging Experiences

Learning and development are the core of early years education, forming the foundation for a child's lifelong journey of discovery. In early years settings, learning is not confined to structured play. Instead, children thrive with playful exploration, hands-on experiences, and meaningful interactions. A well-rounded approach to learning and development focuses on nurturing every aspect of a child's growth—physical, cognitive, emotional and social—ensuring they flourish in an environment tailored to their needs and interests.

Practitioners have a vital role in creating engaging, child-centred experiences that foster curiosity, creativity, and critical thinking. At the same time, they must nurture children's emotional well-being, helping them feel safe, valued, and ready to learn.

Play-Based Learning

Play is the beating heart of early childhood education. It's how children make sense of the world around them, develop essential skills, and express their ideas. Through play, children can explore new concepts, experiment with problem-solving, and build relationships—all in an environment that feels fun and natural.

Learning Through Play

Play provides endless opportunities for development across all areas of learning. Whether it's a child role-playing as a doctor, constructing a tower with blocks, or exploring nature in the garden, these activities develop critical skills such as language, creativity, and resilience. For example, a group of children building a fort together not only strengthens their fine motor skills but also encourages teamwork, negotiation, and imaginative thinking.

Child-Led Learning

Following a child's interests is key to creating meaningful and engaging experiences. When children are given the freedom to explore what fascinates them, their learning becomes self-motivated and more impactful. For example, if a child shows a keen interest in insects, setting up a "mini-beast investigation station" with magnifying glasses, books, and models can spark their curiosity and encourage independent exploration. Child-led learning requires practitioners to be attentive, flexible, and ready to adapt their planning to reflect the children's evolving interests.

A Balanced Curriculum

A high-quality early years curriculum strikes a balance between planned activities and opportunities for free exploration. It should include experiences that stimulate all areas of development while ensuring that children have the time and space to follow their instincts and interests.

Supporting Physical Development

Physical play is an essential part of learning in the early years, helping children develop coordination, strength and confidence. From climbing equipment to obstacle courses and sensory activities like threading or pouring, these experiences build motor skills while promoting a sense of achievement. Outdoor play, in particular, offers opportunities for risk-taking and problem-solving, such as navigating uneven terrain or building a den with natural materials.

Promoting Emotional and Social Growth

The early years are a critical time for developing social and emotional skills. Activities that encourage turn-taking, collaboration, and empathy—like group storytelling, role-play, or cooperative games—help children build positive relationships and develop emotional resilience. Practitioners play a key role in modelling kindness and helping children navigate social challenges, such as resolving conflicts or expressing feelings in constructive ways.

Encouraging Cognitive Development

Cognitive growth in the early years is driven by curiosity and exploration. Activities that involve sorting, counting, or problem-solving help children develop critical thinking and early mathematical skills. For example, a water play station with measuring jugs encourages exploration of volume and concepts like "more" and "less." Similarly, puzzles, building activities, and open-ended resources like loose parts encourage creativity and problem-solving.

Fostering Creativity and Expression

Creativity is at the heart of early learning, giving children the freedom to express themselves and develop confidence in their ideas. Art, music, and role-play provide outlets for self-expression while also promoting fine motor skills, language development, and emotional well-being. For example, providing a range of materials in an art area—paint, collage items, and natural objects—invites children to explore textures, colours, and shapes in their own unique way.

Assessment and Planning for Learning

To support children's development effectively, practitioners need to observe and assess their progress, using this information to plan engaging and purposeful activities.

Observation and Assessment

Regular observations provide valuable insights into what children know, can do, and enjoy. These observations should focus on the whole child, capturing not only their academic progress but also their social, emotional, and physical growth. For example, observing a child who builds elaborate structures with blocks might reveal an emerging interest in engineering or spatial awareness.

Using the Early Years Foundation Stage (EYFS), practitioners can assess whether children are meeting developmental milestones or might benefit from additional support. However, assessments should be holistic and child-focused, avoiding rigid comparisons or pressure to meet benchmarks.

Curriculum in Early Years: Intention, Implementation, and Impact

In the world of early years education, the curriculum forms the foundation for everything we do. It's the map that guides children's learning journeys, ensuring they gain the skills, knowledge, and experiences they need to thrive. But a curriculum isn't just about ticking off developmental milestones—it's about creating a rich, engaging environment that responds to children's needs and interests while keeping clear goals in mind.

At its heart, the curriculum revolves around three key principles:

Intent

Implementation

Impact

These principles ensure that every activity, interaction, and experience has a purpose, is delivered effectively, and contributes to meaningful learning.

Let me break this down for you

Intention: Knowing What You Want Children to Learn (Their next steps)

The intention is the starting point of the curriculum—it's where you define what you want children to learn and why it matters. It's about having a clear vision of the knowledge, skills, and dispositions you want children to develop during their time in your setting.

In early years settings, intentions are often rooted in the Early Years Foundation Stage (EYFS) framework, which outlines the seven areas of learning and development:

1. Communication and Language

2. Physical Development

3. Personal, Social, and Emotional Development

4. Literacy

5. Mathematics

6. Understanding the World

7. Expressive Arts and Design

While these areas provide a structure, intentions go beyond simply covering the framework. They involve understanding the individual and unique needs of the children in your care and identifying what they need to flourish. For example, if a child is shy and struggles to engage with peers, your intention might be to help them build confidence and develop social skills.

Long-Term and Short-Term Intentions

Intentions can be broad and long-term, such as fostering independence or promoting a love of books, or they can be specific and short-term, like helping a child learn to count to five or hold a pencil. A strong curriculum balances these perspectives, ensuring that children are supported in achieving both overarching goals and immediate developmental milestones.

Why Intention Matters

Having clear intentions gives your curriculum focus and purpose. It ensures that every activity, resource, and interaction is meaningful, aligned with what you want children to learn. It also provides a framework for evaluating progress, helping you identify whether children are on track or need additional support.

Intentions should be ambitious yet achievable, reflecting high expectations for what children can learn while remaining realistic and developmentally appropriate. This balance ensures that children are challenged and engaged without feeling overwhelmed.

Implementation: Learning Through Interests and Play

Once you've established clear intentions, the next step is implementation—bringing the curriculum to life. In early years settings, this means creating an environment and experiences that allow children to explore, experiment, and learn in ways that feel natural and enjoyable.

Following Children's Interests

One of the most powerful ways to implement a curriculum in the early years is by tapping into children's interests. When children are excited about a topic, they're naturally more engaged and motivated to learn.

By weaving your intentions into children's interests, you create a curriculum that feels relevant and exciting while still meeting developmental goals.

Implementation also involves tailoring your approach to meet the unique needs of each child. For example, some children might learn best through hands-on activities, while others benefit from visual aids or verbal explanations. Being flexible and responsive ensures that every child has the opportunity to engage with and benefit from the curriculum.

Impact: The Joy of Learning Something New

The final element of the curriculum is impact—seeing the results of your efforts and understanding how children are learning and growing as a result of your intentions and implementation. These moments of progress reflect the success of your curriculum and highlight the value of your work.

A strong curriculum is more than a plan—it's the heart of your setting's practice. By clearly defining what you want children to learn, delivering it in meaningful ways, and celebrating the impact of their learning, you create an environment where every child can thrive.

For practitioners, the curriculum provides a sense of purpose and direction, helping them feel confident and inspired in their work. For families, it demonstrates a commitment to quality and care, reassuring them that their children are in the best hands. And for children, it offers the foundation for a lifetime of learning, exploration, and growth.

Planning for Progress

Planning based on observation and assessment ensures that activities are meaningful and tailored to each child's needs and interests. For example, if a group of children shows a fascination with dinosaurs, practitioners might plan a series of activities around this theme, such as digging for "fossils" in the sandpit, creating dinosaur crafts, or reading books about prehistoric creatures.

Flexibility is key. Plans should be adaptable to allow for spontaneous opportunities, like a child bringing in a special object from home or an unexpected interest emerging during play.

Creating an Enabling Environment

The environment plays a crucial role in supporting learning and development. A well-organised, inviting space encourages exploration, independence, and creativity.

Children should be able to access materials independently, choosing items that spark their interest and inspire their play. For example, open shelving with clearly labelled baskets allows children to select toys, books, or art supplies without needing adult assistance.

Dividing the space into distinct areas—such as a reading corner, sensory station, and construction zone—supports different types of play and learning. Outdoor spaces should be equally stimulating, with opportunities for physical activity, nature exploration, and quiet reflection.Showcasing children's work and ideas on walls or in portfolios celebrates their achievements and reinforces their sense of belonging. For example, a display documenting a recent project on plants, complete with photos, drawings, and children's comments, helps make learning visible and meaningful.

The Role of Relationships in Learning

Learning and development don't happen in isolation—they are shaped by the relationships children have with practitioners, peers, and their families.Warm, responsive relationships between practitioners and children create a foundation of trust and security. When children feel safe and valued, they are more likely to take risks, try new things, and engage deeply in their learning. For example, a practitioner sitting alongside a child as they explore a new puzzle provides encouragement and support, building both confidence and competence.

Engaging Families

Families are children's first educators, and their involvement is crucial to supporting learning and development. Regular communication with parents about their child's progress, interests, and experiences helps create a seamless connection between home and the setting. For example, sharing a child's fascination with trains might inspire parents to visit a train museum or read train-themed books at home, reinforcing the child's learning journey.

Learning and Development in Inspections

During inspections, learning and development are central to the assessment of a setting's quality. Inspectors will look for evidence of a well-balanced curriculum, meaningful observations and assessments, and a stimulating environment that supports children's growth.Practitioners should be able to articulate how they support learning and development, explaining the purpose behind their activities and how they adapt to meet individual needs.

For example, a practitioner might describe how they use water play to introduce mathematical concepts or how they incorporate sensory materials to engage a child with additional needs.

M is for Monitoring

Evaluating and Improving Your Setting

Monitoring is the lifeblood of any high-quality early years setting. It's the process of continually evaluating your practices, identifying areas for improvement, and ensuring that your setting meets the needs of children, families, and staff. Far from being a one-off task or a tick-box exercise, monitoring is an ongoing commitment to excellence. It's about creating a culture of reflection, accountability, and progress, where everyone works together to deliver the best possible outcomes for children.

When done effectively, monitoring provides a clear picture of what's working well and where there's room to grow. It helps you stay inspection-ready at all times, fosters a motivated and well-supported team, and ensures that every child's developmental needs are met. Whether you're tracking children's progress, evaluating staff performance, or auditing your policies and procedures, monitoring is essential to maintaining high standards across your setting.

Monitoring Children's Progress and Development

One of the most critical aspects of monitoring in an early years setting is tracking children's progress and development. This involves observing, assessing, and documenting each child's learning journey, ensuring that they're making progress in line with their individual potential and the Early Years Foundation Stage (EYFS) framework.

Using Observations to Inform Monitoring

Observations are at the heart of monitoring children's progress. By observing children during play and planned activities, practitioners can gather valuable insights into their strengths, interests, and areas where they may need additional support. These observations should be documented systematically, forming the basis for ongoing assessment and planning.

For example, if a practitioner notices that a child consistently struggles with turn-taking during group games, this observation can inform strategies to support their social development. Similarly, if a child shows a keen interest in numbers, practitioners can plan activities that nurture this interest, such as counting games or introducing simple maths concepts through play.

Tracking Developmental Milestones

Monitoring also involves comparing children's progress to developmental milestones. While every child develops at their own pace, milestones provide a useful benchmark for identifying typical progress and spotting potential delays. For instance, if a two-year-old isn't yet combining words into short phrases, practitioners can work with parents and other professionals to explore ways to support their communication skills.

Using tools like progress trackers, learning journals, and the progress check at age two, practitioners can build a comprehensive picture of each child's development. These records not only guide planning but also provide valuable evidence for inspections, demonstrating how the setting supports children's learning and growth.

Engaging Families in Monitoring

Parents are essential partners in monitoring their child's progress. Regular communication with families ensures that practitioners have a holistic view of the child's development, incorporating insights from home as well as the setting. This might involve sharing observations, inviting parents to contribute to learning journals, or discussing progress during parent meetings. By involving families, practitioners can create a shared understanding of the child's needs and work collaboratively to support their development.

Monitoring the Quality of Teaching and Staff Performance

While monitoring children's progress is vital, it's equally important to evaluate the quality of teaching and the performance of your staff team. After all, practitioners are the ones who bring the curriculum to life, and their skills, knowledge, and attitudes have a direct impact on children's experiences and outcomes.

Observing Practice

Regular observations of staff practice are a cornerstone of effective monitoring. These observations should focus on how practitioners interact with children, deliver activities, and support learning. For example, you might observe how a practitioner encourages problem-solving during a construction activity or how they scaffold a child's language development through open-ended questions.

When observing staff, it's important to approach the process with a spirit of support and collaboration rather than criticism. The goal is to identify strengths, celebrate good practice, and provide constructive feedback to help practitioners grow.

Providing Feedback and Support

Feedback is a powerful tool for improving practice, but it needs to be specific, actionable, and delivered in a supportive way. For instance, instead of saying, "You need to improve your group time," you might say, "I noticed the children were restless during group time—what if we tried breaking it into shorter segments or adding a hands-on activity to keep them engaged?"

Regular supervision meetings provide an opportunity to discuss observations, set professional development goals, and address any challenges. These one-to-one conversations help practitioners reflect on their practice, build confidence, and feel valued as part of the team.

Encouraging Peer Learning

Monitoring isn't just the responsibility of leaders—it's something the whole team can engage in through peer observations and shared reflections. For example, staff might observe each other delivering activities and share constructive feedback or ideas. This collaborative approach fosters a culture of learning and improvement, where everyone feels empowered to contribute to the setting's success.

Tracking Professional Development

Monitoring also involves keeping track of staff training and development. This includes ensuring that all mandatory training, such as safeguarding and paediatric first aid, is up-to-date, as well as providing opportunities for practitioners to deepen their knowledge and skills. Whether it's attending workshops, pursuing formal qualifications, or participating in in-house training, professional development is essential for maintaining a high-quality team.

N is for Nutrition

Nurturing Healthy Bodies and Minds

Good nutrition in early childhood lays the foundation for lifelong health, growth and learning. It's about more than simply providing healthy food—it's about creating an environment where children develop a positive relationship with food and understand the role it plays in keeping their bodies and minds strong. Early years are critical for instilling habits that children will carry with them for the rest of their lives, making the role of practitioners in this process all the more important.

A thoughtful approach to nutrition supports physical development, enhances concentration, and contributes to emotional well-being. Proper nutrition affects every aspect of a child's day—from their energy levels during play to their ability to focus on learning tasks. By creating mealtimes that are nutritious, engaging, and inclusive, early years settings can foster an environment where healthy eating is not only encouraged but celebrated. A commitment to good nutrition isn't just about meeting guidelines; it's about empowering children with the tools to make informed choices that will benefit them for years to come.

Balanced and Nutritious Meals

A varied and wholesome diet is key to supporting children's growth and development. Meals and snacks should be carefully planned to include all the essential nutrients, with a balance of fruits, vegetables, proteins, whole grains, and dairy. For instance, colourful fruits and vegetables not only provide key vitamins and minerals but also make meals more visually appealing, encouraging even the pickiest eaters to try new foods. Whole grains help maintain steady energy levels throughout the day, while proteins support muscle and tissue growth—both essential for active, growing children.

Reducing processed foods and added sugars is vital in maintaining children's overall health. Sugary foods can lead to energy spikes and crashes, making it harder for children to focus during structured activities. On the other hand, a well-balanced diet helps regulate their energy, mood, and concentration, creating the optimal conditions for learning and play.

For settings that provide meals, collaboration with nutritionists or adherence to recognised dietary guidelines can ensure that menus meet the nutritional needs of young children. Planning meals seasonally can also add variety and ensure ingredients are fresh and high quality. For instance, hearty vegetable soups in winter or fresh fruit salads in summer not only align with seasonal produce but also teach children about the natural cycles of food. How about encouraging children to make their own soup for their lunch?

Catering to individual dietary requirements is an essential part of an inclusive approach to nutrition. Whether it's managing allergies, religious or cultural dietary restrictions, or personal preferences such as vegetarian or vegan diets, clear communication and robust systems are key. Allergy management, in particular, requires meticulous attention to detail, including clear labelling of meals, separate preparation areas to prevent cross-contamination, and a thorough understanding of each child's specific needs. Alternative meals should be just as nutritionally balanced and visually appealing as the main menu, ensuring that no child feels left out during mealtimes.

Mealtime as a Learning Experience

Mealtimes are far more than just opportunities to refuel—they are valuable moments for socialisation, education and skill-building. By encouraging children to engage with their food and understand where it comes from, practitioners can lay the groundwork for a lifelong appreciation of healthy eating. This is so important and I highly recommend that you as practitioners use this as learning opportunities for children. Rather than a tick box exercise to contain children. How about encouraging rolling lunch? I have seen this on several occasions and I have to say it is one of the most awesome learning opportunities I have ever seen.

Teaching Healthy Habits

Early childhood is the perfect time to introduce children to concepts such as portion control, balanced diets, and the benefits of trying new foods. These lessons can be woven into mealtime conversations in a fun and engaging way. For example, practitioners might explain that eating a rainbow of vegetables provides "superpowers" like strength, energy, and sharp minds. Turning nutrition into an exciting narrative helps children associate healthy eating with positive outcomes.

Stories about where food comes from—such as how carrots grow underground or how milk comes from cows—can also spark curiosity and deepen children's connection to their meals. These discussions can be enhanced by hands-on activities, such as growing herbs or vegetables in a garden, which allow children to see the journey from seed to plate.

Encouraging Independence

Mealtimes are also an opportunity to foster independence and decision-making skills. Where appropriate, allowing children to serve themselves or choose their portions helps them develop autonomy and self-regulation. For example, a child might use tongs to pick items from a serving bowl or pour water into their own cup. Practitioners can guide these activities by encouraging children to make balanced choices, such as adding both vegetables and grains to their plate, while still respecting their preferences. Please do not say that you do this if it is not happening every time children sit down to eat.

These small acts of independence not only build confidence but also help children develop a healthy relationship with food. Allowing them to listen to their hunger cues, rather than enforcing a clean plate rule, encourages mindful eating and reduces the risk of overeating habits later in life.

Fluids and Snacks

Proper hydration is just as important as balanced meals for supporting children's health and well-being. Water should always be readily available throughout the day, with regular reminders to drink, particularly during physical activities or warmer weather. Dehydration can lead to fatigue, irritability, and difficulty concentrating, so promoting hydration is crucial. Using colourful cups or water bottles can make drinking water more appealing for young children and encourage them to stay hydrated.

Snacks play an important role in maintaining energy levels between meals. Fresh fruit, vegetable sticks, wholegrain crackers, and yoghurt are excellent options that provide a balance of nutrients without being overly heavy. Avoiding sugary or processed snacks helps prevent the energy crashes often associated with high sugar intake. Structured snack times ensure children receive consistent nutrition while maintaining a predictable routine, which is comforting for young learners.

Creating a Positive Mealtime Environment

The atmosphere during mealtimes is just as important as the food itself. A calm, well-organised setting encourages children to eat at their own pace and enjoy their meals without feeling rushed or pressured.

Sitting together at a table promotes social interaction, providing opportunities for children to practise conversational skills, share their experiences, and observe positive eating behaviours in their peers.

Practitioners play a key role in shaping the mealtime environment. By sitting with the children, modelling healthy eating habits, and engaging in positive conversations about food, practitioners can influence children's attitudes toward nutrition. For instance, talking about the crunch of a carrot or the sweetness of an apple makes eating a sensory experience, sparking curiosity and enjoyment.

Creating a predictable mealtime routine—complete with consistent seating arrangements and familiar utensils—fosters a sense of security. For children who are hesitant eaters, this consistency can help reduce anxiety and create a more enjoyable dining experience.

Involving Families in Nutrition

Parents are a child's first teachers when it comes to nutrition, so involving them in your setting's approach to healthy eating can strengthen the home-setting connection. Sharing weekly menus, providing recipe ideas, or hosting workshops on nutrition empowers families to make informed choices at home. These initiatives create continuity between the setting and the home, reinforcing positive eating habits in both environments.

Clear and open communication about allergies, dietary preferences, and cultural or religious food requirements is essential. Parents need to feel confident that their child's needs are being met with care and attention. This trust fosters stronger relationships and reassures families that their children are in a supportive and inclusive environment.

Nutrition and Inspections

During inspections, lunch times and nutrition often comes under scrutiny, as it plays a vital role in supporting children's health and development. Inspectors will review menus, observe how dietary requirements are managed, and assess the overall mealtime environment. Demonstrating that your setting is committed to providing high-quality nutrition involves keeping detailed records of menus, allergy management procedures, and food hygiene practices.

Additionally, inspectors are likely to observe how mealtimes are used as opportunities for learning and social interaction. For example, they might note how practitioners encourage children to engage with their food, foster independence, and model positive attitudes. A strong focus on nutrition reflects your setting's dedication to holistic child development, which will leave a lasting impression during inspections.

Why Nutrition Matters

Nutrition in early years settings is about so much more than meeting basic needs—it's about nurturing healthy bodies and minds. A balanced diet supports children's growth, fuels their learning, and lays the groundwork for lifelong health. By creating an environment that celebrates food, teaches positive habits, and respects individual needs, early years settings can instil a love for healthy eating that children will carry into adulthood.

The impact of good nutrition extends beyond the individual child, influencing the well-being of families and the broader community. When children are well-nourished, they are better equipped to engage with their peers, absorb new information, and enjoy their childhood to the fullest. For practitioners, investing time and energy into promoting nutrition is one of the most meaningful ways to support children's development and prepare them for a bright future.

O is for Observations

The Foundation of Learning and Development

Observations are the cornerstone of early years practice. They allow practitioners to understand children's interests, assess their developmental progress, and plan activities that nurture growth. But for observations to have real impact, they must be robust, secure, and used effectively. Robust observations provide accurate insights into what children know, can do, and enjoy, while secure handling ensures that sensitive information is protected and used responsibly.

In an inspection, the quality of your observations can be a make-or-break factor. Inspectors will want to see how well you know the children in your care, how you use observations to plan learning, and how you document this process. But beyond inspections, effective observations are crucial for building a child-centred approach, creating meaningful experiences, and forming strong partnerships with families.

What Are Observations?

Observations are the process of watching, listening, and reflecting on what children do and say. They provide a window into a child's world, capturing moments of learning, play, and interaction. These insights help practitioners:

- Understand each child's developmental stage.
- Recognise their interests, strengths, and areas for development.
- Plan activities that are tailored to their needs.

For example, if you observe a child repeatedly stacking blocks, you might conclude they're exploring concepts like balance, structure, and problem-solving. This could inform your planning, leading you to introduce more complex building challenges or books about construction.

The Importance of Robust Observations

Robust observations are thorough, accurate, and meaningful. They go beyond surface-level descriptions to provide a deep understanding of a child's development and learning. Here's why robust observations are so important:

1. Capturing the Whole Child

Every child is unique, with their own interests, strengths, and challenges. Robust observations provide a holistic view of each child, ensuring that their individuality is recognised and supported.

For instance, a single observation of a child painting might reveal not just their artistic interest but also their fine motor skills, concentration, and willingness to try new things. This level of detail allows you to plan activities that nurture all aspects of their development.

2. Supporting Accurate Assessment

Observations form the basis of assessment, helping you track progress against developmental milestones. By documenting what children can do, you can identify whether they're on track or need additional support.

For example, a series of observations might show that a child is struggling with turn-taking during group play. This insight could lead to targeted interventions, such as introducing cooperative games or modelling social skills.

3. Informing Planning

Robust observations ensure that planning is purposeful and child-centred. By understanding what children enjoy and what they need to learn, you can create activities that are engaging, meaningful, and developmentally appropriate.

For instance, if a child shows an interest in dinosaurs, you could plan activities that explore different learning areas, such as counting dinosaur footprints (maths), creating a dino-themed sensory bin (fine motor skills), or reading books about prehistoric creatures (literacy).

Building Strong Relationships

Observations help you connect with children on a deeper level. By tuning into their interests and recognising their achievements, you build trust and create an environment where they feel valued and understood.

How to Make Observations Robust

Robust observations require skill, attention to detail, and a clear purpose. Here are some tips for making your observations more effective:

Focus on the Child's Actions and Words

Describe what the child does and says in detail, avoiding assumptions or interpretations. For example, instead of writing "Tommy is happy painting," describe the child's actions: "Tommy used a thick brush to make wide blue strokes across the paper, smiling and saying, 'I'm making the sky.'" This approach provides a more accurate picture of the child's behaviour and learning.

Use Different Observation Methods

Mix up your methods to capture a well-rounded view of the child. Some common types of observations include:

Narrative Observations: A detailed account of a child's activity over a set period.

Snapshot Observations: A quick record of a single moment.

Targeted Observations: Focused on a specific area of development, such as language or physical skills.

Photographic or Video Observations: Visual records that complement written notes.

Link Observations to Developmental Goals

Connect your observations to the Early Years Foundation Stage (EYFS) framework or other developmental guidelines. This helps you identify where children are excelling and where they may need additional support. For example, an observation of a child threading beads could be linked to the EYFS goal of developing fine motor skills and hand-eye coordination.

Be Consistent

Consistency is key to building a complete picture of each child's development. Make observations regularly and ensure they cover all areas of learning and development over time. This ensures that no aspect of the child's growth is overlooked.

Using Observations to Engage Families

Observations are a valuable tool for building partnerships with parents. By sharing insights into their child's development, you can create a shared understanding of their progress and needs.

Sharing Learning Journeys

Many settings use learning journals to document and share observations with families. These journals provide a rich record of the child's experiences, helping parents see how their child is growing and learning.

For example, a learning journal might include photos, notes, and samples of the child's work, along with explanations of how these activities support their development.

Encouraging Parent Contributions

Invite parents to contribute their own observations to the learning journey. For instance, they might share photos or notes about milestones at home, such as a child learning to ride a bike or recognising letters in their name.

P is for Partnerships

Building Strong Relationships with Parents, Professionals, and the Community

In early years education, partnerships are the glue that holds everything together. By fostering strong connections with parents, outside agencies, other settings, and the wider community, you create a collaborative and supportive network that benefits children in every aspect of their development. Effective partnerships ensure that children feel secure, families feel valued, and practitioners have the tools and insights to provide the best possible care.

Partnerships are not one-size-fits-all; they are built on trust, mutual respect, and open communication. Whether it's a daily chat with a parent, a joint intervention plan with a speech therapist, or shared training with another local setting, partnerships create opportunities for consistency, enriched experiences, and holistic support for every child.

Partnerships with Parents

Parents are a child's first educators, and working in partnership with them is fundamental to supporting children's learning and well-being. A strong relationship with parents builds trust, creates consistency between home and the setting, and empowers families to play an active role in their child's development.

Open Communication

Establishing clear and regular communication is the foundation of a strong parent partnership. Daily handovers, newsletters, and digital platforms like apps or emails keep parents informed about their child's experiences and progress. Sharing details of activities, meals, or learning milestones reassures parents and helps them feel connected to their child's day.

Listening is just as important as sharing. Providing opportunities for parents to voice their concerns, ask questions, or share insights about their child fosters a collaborative relationship. For example, regular parent meetings or informal coffee mornings or stay and play can open the door to meaningful conversations.

Involving Parents in Learning

Encouraging parents to take an active role in their child's learning journey strengthens the bond between home and the setting. Simple strategies, like asking parents to share observations from home or inviting them to contribute to their child's learning journal, ensure that their input is valued.

Workshops or resources on topics such as play-based learning, early literacy, or managing behaviour at home can empower parents with the tools to support their child's development. For example, a workshop on reading aloud might inspire parents to introduce bedtime stories, reinforcing skills and interests nurtured in the setting.

Collaborating with the Community

The wider community offers a wealth of opportunities to enrich children's experiences and broaden their horizons. Engaging with local people, places, and organisations helps children feel part of something bigger while fostering curiosity and social connections.

Building Community Connections

Connecting with the local community adds depth and variety to children's learning. Visits from community professionals—like firefighters, librarians, or local artists—introduce children to different roles and experiences, sparking interest and building understanding. Trips to parks, shops, or farms allow children to explore their surroundings and develop a sense of place.

Participating in local events, such as fairs or charity fundraisers, strengthens the setting's role in the community while teaching children about collaboration and contribution. These experiences foster a sense of belonging and help children understand the world beyond their immediate environment.

Partnerships with External Professionals

Working with external specialists, such as speech therapists, occupational therapists, health visitors, or educational psychologists, ensures that children receive tailored support to meet their individual needs. These professionals bring expertise and insights that complement the work of the setting, helping practitioners implement targeted interventions.

For instance, a speech therapist might provide strategies for supporting a child's language development, while an educational psychologist could offer guidance on managing behavioural challenges. Regular communication and collaboration with these professionals ensure that support plans are consistent and effective, creating a seamless experience for the child and their family.

Partnerships with Other Settings

Collaborating with other early years settings or schools strengthens the continuity of care and learning for children. Sharing ideas, resources, or training opportunities helps practitioners stay informed and inspired while ensuring smooth transitions for children.

Networking with other settings can provide access to shared training sessions or resources, such as guest speakers or workshops. For example, pooling resources for a session on outdoor learning might benefit multiple teams and create opportunities for sharing best practices.

Transition Support

When children move between settings—such as from nursery to school—strong partnerships between providers ensure that transitions are smooth and positive. Sharing developmental records, meeting with teachers, and preparing children through activities like role-play or "school visits" all contribute to a sense of readiness and confidence.

Supporting Transitions

Transitions are significant moments for children and their families, and effective partnerships are key to making these as smooth as possible.

For children starting in a setting, the transition from home can be daunting. Offering settling-in sessions, where parents stay to ease their child into the environment, can make the process less overwhelming. Home visits before a child starts can also provide valuable insights into their routines, preferences, and personality, helping practitioners tailor their approach. This is exactly the same when a child moves from one room to another.

The move to school is another major transition, and partnerships with local schools are vital in preparing children for this step. Sharing developmental information, hosting visits from reception teachers, and introducing activities that mirror school routines—like sitting for longer group sessions—help children feel prepared. Strong communication with parents throughout the process ensures they feel confident and supported.

Partnerships Among Staff

Effective partnerships aren't limited to external relationships—they also thrive within the setting itself. A cohesive team that communicates openly and supports one another creates a positive environment for everyone.

Regular staff meetings, peer observations, and opportunities for reflective practice foster collaboration and ensure that everyone is working towards the same goals. For example, a weekly discussion about children's progress might highlight shared strategies for supporting a child who's struggling with separation anxiety.

Mentoring and coaching between more experienced and newer team members can also strengthen internal partnerships, building skills and confidence across the team.

Partnerships and Inspections

Inspectors place a high value on partnerships, as they demonstrate the setting's commitment to collaboration and holistic care. Evidence of parent engagement, such as learning journals, meeting minutes, or feedback surveys, shows that families are actively involved.

Records of collaboration with external professionals, such as intervention plans or reports from specialists, highlight the setting's proactive approach to meeting children's needs. For community partnerships, photos, newsletters, or documentation of events can showcase the richness of the setting's connections.

During inspections, practitioners should be able to articulate how these partnerships enhance children's experiences and contribute to their overall development.

Q is for Quality Assurance

Maintaining High Standards Across Your Setting

Quality assurance is the backbone of a successful early years setting, ensuring that high standards are consistently met across all areas of care and education. It's not just about meeting regulatory requirements—it's about striving for excellence in everything you do, from teaching practices to safety measures, and creating a setting where children thrive, parents feel confident, and staff are proud of their work.

At its heart, quality assurance is an ongoing process of reflection, evaluation, and improvement. It's about asking, "What's working well? What can we do better?" and taking meaningful steps to address those questions. When quality assurance becomes embedded in your setting's culture, it creates a cycle of continuous improvement that benefits everyone.

Self-Evaluation and Reflection

Self-evaluation is the cornerstone of quality assurance, providing a structured way to review your setting's performance and identify areas for growth.

Regular self-assessment ensures that your setting stays on track and remains aligned with best practices in early years education. A structured self-evaluation can be a valuable tool for documenting strengths, weaknesses, and plans for improvement. For example, you might reflect on how well your environment supports child-led learning or whether staff feel confident in implementing new safeguarding protocols.

Self-evaluation should go beyond ticking boxes—it's about meaningful reflection. Observing children's engagement, analysing staff practices, and reviewing outcomes for children all provide insights that help shape your approach. By consistently reflecting on what's working and what could be better, you create a setting that's responsive and dynamic.

Involving the Team

Quality assurance is a collective effort. Involving all staff in the evaluation process ensures that everyone has a voice and feels invested in maintaining high standards. Team meetings, reflective discussions, and peer observations are all opportunities to share insights and ideas. For instance, a practitioner might highlight how rearranging a play area improved engagement, sparking a wider conversation about optimising the learning environment.

Creating a culture of shared responsibility promotes accountability and encourages staff to take ownership of their contributions to the setting's success.

Parent and Staff Feedback

Feedback from parents and staff is a vital part of the quality assurance process. These perspectives provide valuable insights into how well your setting meets the needs of children and families and highlight areas where improvements can be made.

Gathering Feedback

Use a variety of methods to gather feedback, such as surveys, suggestion boxes, or informal chats during drop-off and pick-up times. Parents might offer insights into how their child experiences the setting, while staff can provide feedback on everything from training needs to the effectiveness of policies. For example, a parent survey might reveal a desire for more outdoor activities, prompting a review of your outdoor play provision.

Collaboration with Parents

Parents are key stakeholders in your setting's success, and their involvement strengthens the quality assurance process. Inviting parents to share their observations or contribute ideas demonstrates that their opinions are valued. For instance, hosting a "parent forum" where families can discuss the setting's approach to learning and care creates opportunities for collaboration and trust-building.

Actively responding to feedback—whether by making changes or explaining why certain practices are in place—shows a commitment to continuous improvement.

Quality Improvement Plans

Quality assurance isn't just about identifying areas for improvement; it's about taking action. Quality improvement plans (QIPs) provide a clear roadmap for implementing changes and tracking progress.

An effective QIP outlines specific goals, strategies, and timelines for addressing areas that need development. For example, if observations reveal that children aren't engaging with the reading corner, your action plan might include reorganising the space, introducing new books, and monitoring the impact over time.

Having a clear, documented plan ensures that improvements are made systematically rather than reactively. It also provides a sense of direction for the team, helping everyone stay focused on shared goals.

Regularly reviewing your QIP keeps the momentum going and ensures that changes are effective. This might involve team discussions about what's working, challenges encountered, and next steps. For example, if a training session on inclusive practices was part of your action plan, you could follow up with peer observations to see how the strategies are being applied in practice.

Partnerships in Quality Assurance

Quality assurance thrives on collaboration, not just within your setting but also with external partners.

Engaging with external professionals, such as local authority advisors, early years consultants, or safeguarding leads, can provide valuable support and fresh perspectives. These partnerships ensure that your practices remain aligned with current regulations and best practices. For example, a safeguarding advisor might review your policies and recommend updates to reflect new guidance.

Collaborating with other early years settings offers opportunities for shared learning and improvement. For example, visiting another nursery to see how they manage transitions or deliver outdoor learning might inspire new approaches in your own setting. Regular networking and knowledge-sharing strengthen quality across the sector.

Inspections are a key moment to demonstrate the strength of your quality assurance processes. Inspectors will want to see clear evidence of how you monitor, evaluate, and improve your provision.

Documentation is crucial during inspections. This includes your SEF, QIP, staff training records and parent feedback. Being able to show how feedback informs changes and how improvements are tracked highlights your proactive approach.

For example, if your QIP includes a goal to enhance outdoor play, inspectors will want to see evidence of what actions were taken—perhaps introducing new equipment or planning outdoor learning activities—and the impact these changes had on children's engagement and development.

Inspectors will also observe how staff articulate their role in maintaining quality. Practitioners should be able to explain how they contribute to the setting's goals, whether it's through reflective practice, professional development, or engaging with parents. Confident, knowledgeable staff are a clear indicator of a setting committed to excellence.

The Impact of Quality Assurance

Quality assurance isn't just about meeting standards—it's about exceeding them. A robust approach creates a setting where children are engaged, families are satisfied, and staff are empowered. It builds a culture of pride and professionalism, where everyone is working towards the same goal: providing the best possible care and education.

When quality assurance is embedded in daily practice, it becomes second nature. It drives innovation, strengthens relationships, and ensures that your setting remains a place of growth and inspiration for everyone involved.

R is for Resources

Providing High-Quality Tools for Learning and Development

The resources in an early years setting are much more than toys and tools—they're the building blocks of meaningful learning experiences. Carefully chosen, high-quality resources spark curiosity, foster creativity, and support holistic development across all areas of the Early Years Foundation Stage (EYFS) framework. From open-ended materials that inspire imaginative play to diverse resources that promote inclusion, the materials in your setting play a pivotal role in shaping how children learn, explore, and grow.

When resources are thoughtfully selected and organised, they empower children to make independent choices, engage in self-directed learning, and build confidence in their abilities. High-quality resources also create an inviting, stimulating environment that supports both child-led exploration and structured activities, helping practitioners meet the developmental needs of every child in their care.

Age-Appropriate and Open-Ended Resources

Providing resources that cater to all areas of the EYFS framework is essential for fostering well-rounded development. Carefully selected materials can support communication and language, physical development, and personal, social, and emotional growth. For example, books, puppets and storytelling props help children expand their vocabulary and explore narrative skills, while physical resources like climbing frames and balance beams encourage gross motor development. Smaller tools, such as threading beads or tweezers, refine fine motor skills and build hand-eye coordination.

Role-play items, such as costumes or child-sized kitchen sets, enable children to explore different roles, enhancing their social skills and understanding of the world. Art supplies and sensory materials, like playdough or sand, provide creative outlets for children to express themselves, explore textures, and experiment with problem-solving techniques. By offering a variety of resources that align with different developmental domains, practitioners can create a balanced and engaging learning environment.

Open-ended resources are particularly valuable because they allow children to use their imaginations and think critically. Items like wooden blocks, loose parts (e.g., shells, stones, or bottle caps), and water play equipment can be adapted for countless activities. For instance, blocks might become a castle one day and a bridge the next, helping children develop spatial awareness, balance, and creativity. These versatile materials encourage children to explore their ideas freely, supporting cognitive development and fostering a sense of independence.

Promoting Independence

The way resources are presented is just as important as the resources themselves. Organising materials on low, easily accessible shelves encourages children to make independent choices about their play and learning. Clearly labelled containers—with pictures, words, or both—help children identify where items belong, supporting their ability to tidy up after activities. This organisation not only promotes independence but also reinforces skills such as sorting and categorisation.

Creating areas for different types of play, such as a construction zone, a sensory corner, or a quiet reading nook, makes it easier for children to transition between activities. (These do not need to be labelled though) These distinct spaces allow children to explore their interests, choose activities that align with their mood, and engage in self-directed learning. Fostering independence in this way builds confidence, decision-making skills and a sense of ownership over their environment.

Diverse and Inclusive Resources

Inclusion begins with ensuring that every child feels represented in the resources available in your setting. Books, dolls, puzzles, and games should reflect the diverse cultures, languages, and family structures within your community. For example, a bookshelf featuring stories with characters of different ethnicities, abilities, and family dynamics sends a clear message that all children are valued and welcome.

Resources that celebrate various traditions, festivals and ways of life can help children develop respect and empathy for others. For instance, including books about celebrations like Eid, Hanukkah and Diwali, or providing a dollhouse family set with wheelchair users, encourages children to explore the wider world. This diversity not only enriches children's understanding but also lays the groundwork for a more inclusive mindset.

Adaptive Resources for SEND

Supporting children with special educational needs and disabilities (SEND) requires a thoughtful selection of adaptive resources. Sensory toys, such as textured balls, fidget tools, or weighted blankets, can help children with sensory processing needs feel calm and focused. Visual aids, such as communication boards or visual timetables, provide structure and clarity for children who benefit from additional support in transitioning between activities.

Inclusive resources like large-print books, tactile puzzles, or adjustable seating ensure all children can participate fully in learning experiences. Providing these resources not only meets the needs of individual children but also fosters a sense of belonging. When every child has access to the tools they need to succeed, they feel valued, supported and included within the group.

Sustainable and Natural Materials

Incorporating natural materials into your setting benefits both children and the environment. Items such as wooden toys, shells, stones, and plants offer sensory-rich experiences that encourage exploration and creativity. For example, a basket of pinecones might inspire sorting and counting activities, while a mud kitchen in the outdoor play area invites imaginative role-play.

Natural materials also have a calming aesthetic that can support children's emotional well-being. The tactile and visual qualities of wood, stone and fabric are often more soothing than brightly coloured plastics, creating a more relaxed and engaging learning environment.

Teaching Sustainability

Using eco-friendly resources provides an opportunity to teach children about sustainability. Upcycling materials, such as turning cardboard boxes into imaginative play props or using old jars for craft activities, teaches children about reusing and reducing waste. These activities not only inspire creativity but also instil a sense of responsibility for the environment.

Involving children in recycling activities or creating a compost bin for food scraps introduces them to practical ways they can care for the planet. Practitioners can use these moments to discuss topics like reducing plastic waste or conserving energy, fostering an early awareness of environmental issues.

The Role of Practitioners in Resource Management

Practitioners play a crucial role in ensuring resources meet children's developmental needs. Observing how children interact with materials provides valuable insights into their interests and learning styles. For instance, if children show a fascination with vehicles, practitioners might introduce related books, puzzles, or role-play items to extend their learning.

Rotating resources keeps the environment fresh and exciting, re-engaging children's curiosity and ensuring different areas of learning are consistently supported.

Maintaining Quality and Safety

High-quality resources must be safe, well-maintained, and hygienic. Broken or worn items should be repaired or replaced promptly to avoid frustration or accidents. Practitioners should also establish regular cleaning routines, particularly for shared materials like toys, books, and sensory items. Maintaining a clean, safe environment ensures resources remain inviting and ready for use.

Involving Parents

Parents are valuable partners in resource provision. Inviting families to donate outgrown toys, books, or art supplies not only enriches the setting but also strengthens the connection between home and nursery. Sharing ideas for creative play or lending story sacks for use at home encourages families to extend learning beyond the setting, building continuity between home and setting.

Collaborating with the Community

Local businesses, libraries and charities can provide additional resources or funding. For instance, a partnership with a library might give access to a wider range of books, while local artists or craftspeople could lead workshops or donate materials. Community collaboration enhances the variety and quality of resources available, even on a limited budget.

Networking with other early years settings also opens opportunities to share or swap resources, particularly for specialist items like outdoor equipment or sensory tools. Collaborative partnerships help ensure all settings can offer rich learning environments.

Resources and Inspections

During inspections, the quality and variety of resources are key indicators of how well a setting supports children's learning and development. Inspectors will look for evidence that resources are diverse, inclusive and aligned with the EYFS framework.

Demonstrating how resources promote independence, reflect children's interests, and meet individual needs highlights your setting's commitment to high-quality provision. Keeping detailed records of resource audits, maintenance schedules, and partnerships with parents or the community provides further evidence of effective resource management.

The resources in an early years setting shape every aspect of a child's learning journey. From supporting developmental milestones to fostering creativity and independence, the right tools empower children to explore their world with confidence. By prioritising inclusivity, sustainability, and quality, practitioners create an environment where every child can thrive.

Investing in high-quality resources is an investment in the future—both for the children who use them and the wider community that benefits from their growth and learning. A thoughtful approach to resource provision ensures that early years settings are places of opportunity, discovery, and joy.

S is for Safeguarding

Protecting Children and Creating a Culture of Safety

Safeguarding is the cornerstone of any early years setting, underpinning every aspect of practice. It is the most critical responsibility for practitioners, managers, and leaders, ensuring that children are protected from harm, feel valued, and grow in an environment of trust and security. Safeguarding isn't just about having policies on paper—it's about creating a culture where safety is embedded in daily life, and everyone takes proactive responsibility for protecting children.

Professional curiosity, an awareness of local safeguarding trends, and the ability to build trusting relationships are essential to maintaining the highest standards of safeguarding. Every interaction, observation, and decision contributes to creating an environment where children can thrive safely. When safeguarding is prioritised, children are empowered to explore, learn, and grow in a secure and nurturing environment.

Core Aspects of Safeguarding

Safeguarding encompasses a range of responsibilities that extend far beyond the obvious. It requires vigilance, knowledge and a commitment to ongoing learning to stay abreast of evolving challenges.

Robust Policies and Procedures

A strong safeguarding policy is the foundation of a safe setting. It must clearly outline procedures for identifying and reporting concerns, recognising signs of abuse, neglect, or exploitation, and managing allegations against staff. The policy should also include protocols for maintaining confidentiality, ensuring sensitive information is shared only on a need-to-know basis.

All staff should be familiar with the safeguarding policy and know their role within it. Induction processes must include thorough safeguarding training, ensuring that new staff understand the procedures from day one. Policies should be regularly reviewed and updated to reflect current legislation and guidance, such as the latest updates to *Keeping Children Safe in Education 2024*. This is so important to keep your policy up to date.

Staff Training and Awareness

Regular safeguarding training is essential to keep staff up-to-date on how to spot and respond to concerns. Training should cover topics such as recognising signs of abuse or neglect, understanding specific safeguarding issues like online safety or radicalisation, and knowing the steps to escalate concerns.

Training must also encourage professional curiosity—a mindset of questioning and exploring underlying reasons behind behaviours or circumstances. For example, a child frequently arriving with unexplained injuries or consistently tired might prompt deeper investigation, ensuring that no potential risk is overlooked. Practitioners should also receive updates on local safeguarding trends, such as increased instances of domestic abuse or child exploitation, to tailor their vigilance to current risks.

Safer Recruitment

Every setting must use safer recruitment practices to ensure that all staff are suitable for working with children. This includes conducting enhanced DBS checks, verifying references, and using thorough interview processes to explore candidates' understanding of safeguarding. Clear protocols should be in place for addressing any concerns that arise during these checks or throughout employment. Staff who recruit must have safer recruitment training and follow bets practices.

Beyond initial recruitment, safeguarding measures should extend to ongoing monitoring, including regular supervision and appraisals, to ensure that staff continue to uphold the highest standards of child protection.

Empowering Children

Safeguarding isn't just about protecting children—it's also about equipping them with the knowledge and confidence to protect themselves. Teaching children about personal safety in age-appropriate ways helps them understand boundaries, identify trusted adults, and know when to seek help.

Through storytelling, role-play, or circle-time discussions, practitioners can introduce concepts like privacy, safe touch, and the difference between secrets and surprises. For example, explaining that their bodies belong to them and that it's okay to talk to an adult if something feels wrong helps build resilience and awareness.

The Role of the Designated Safeguarding Lead (DSL)

The Designated Safeguarding Lead (DSL) plays a pivotal role in safeguarding practices. This individual is the main point of contact for safeguarding concerns and is responsible for ensuring the setting's safeguarding policies are effectively implemented.

Key Responsibilities of the DSL

- Managing Concerns: The DSL must assess and act on any safeguarding concerns raised by staff, escalating them to external agencies like children's services when necessary.
- Providing Support and Guidance: Staff members often turn to the DSL for advice on recognising signs of abuse or managing disclosures. The DSL must be approachable, knowledgeable, and confident in offering support.
- Training and Supervision: The DSL ensures that all staff receive regular safeguarding training and understand their roles in protecting children.

- Maintaining Records: Accurate, confidential record-keeping is essential. The DSL must document safeguarding concerns, actions taken, and any communications with external agencies.
- Building Partnerships: The DSL liaises with external agencies, parents, and professionals to ensure a coordinated approach to safeguarding.

The DSL's role is critical in creating a culture of safety. They must model best practices, stay informed about updates in safeguarding guidance, and ensure that the setting remains compliant with legal and ethical obligations.

Operation Encompass

Operation Encompass is a vital initiative that supports children exposed to domestic abuse. It ensures that when the police are called to a domestic incident, schools and early years settings are notified before the start of the next day.

The designated safeguarding lead is informed by the police of the incident, providing essential context to support the child. This early notification allows the setting to take appropriate steps, such as offering additional emotional support, monitoring behaviour, or liaising with other professionals. You can only say you are an Operation Encompass setting if your DSL has completed the free online key adult training.

Why Operation Encompass Matters

Children exposed to domestic abuse often experience trauma that affects their emotional well-being, behaviour, and ability to engage in learning. By participating in Operation Encompass, settings can respond sensitively and proactively, helping children feel secure and supported. This initiative highlights the importance of multi-agency collaboration in safeguarding and the critical role early years practitioners play in a child's recovery.

Creating a Safe Space

Physical Safety

Regular risk assessments are essential for maintaining a safe environment. This includes assessing indoor and outdoor spaces, equipment, and routines to identify and minimise hazards. For example, checking that gates are secure, toys are age-appropriate, and first-aid kits are fully stocked ensures that risks are proactively managed.

Robust procedures for managing access to the setting, such as visitor sign-in systems and locked entryways, protect against unauthorised access. Regular fire drills and lock down practices as well as clear evacuation plans further contribute to children's physical safety.

Emotional Safety

Emotional safety is just as important as physical safety. Practitioners must build trusting relationships with children so that they feel comfortable sharing worries or seeking help. A nurturing environment where children are listened to, respected, and valued helps them develop confidence and resilience.

For example, creating a quiet, cosy corner where children can retreat if they feel overwhelmed provides a sense of security and emotional support. Practitioners should also be empathetic and approachable, reinforcing the message that children's feelings and concerns matter.

Professional Curiosity

Professional curiosity is an indispensable skill in safeguarding, forming the foundation for proactive and effective child protection. It involves being inquisitive and analytical, going beyond surface-level observations to explore the underlying context of what practitioners see and hear. Rather than accepting information or situations at face value, professional curiosity encourages practitioners to dig deeper, question inconsistencies, and seek clarity when something doesn't seem quite right.

This approach is particularly vital when subtle signs of abuse, neglect or exploitation might otherwise be overlooked. For instance, noticing that a child consistently appears tired, withdrawn, or unusually anxious should prompt further exploration. Instead of dismissing these behaviours as isolated incidents, practitioners should consider the potential reasons behind them, such as issues at home, exposure to trauma, or unmet needs. Asking open-ended questions, gently probing for more information, and observing patterns over time are key elements of professional curiosity that can uncover hidden risks.

Practitioners must balance this inquisitiveness with sensitivity and professionalism, ensuring that their approach does not alienate families or create unnecessary tension. Building trusting relationships with both children and parents can make it easier to ask the right questions and gather essential insights, while maintaining a clear focus on the child's well-being.

Understanding Local Safeguarding Trends

In addition to honing professional curiosity, practitioners must stay informed about local safeguarding trends, as risks to children can vary significantly by region. Issues such as county lines activity, online exploitation or increases in domestic abuse may affect some communities more than others, depending on local circumstances. Recognising these trends equips practitioners to be more vigilant and to tailor their safeguarding efforts to address the specific challenges faced by children in their setting.

For example, in areas where county lines drug trafficking is prevalent, practitioners might pay closer attention to signs that a child which may include the siblings is being groomed or coerced, such as sudden absences, unexplained possessions, or associations with older individuals. Similarly, in regions experiencing high levels of domestic abuse, practitioners should be alert to behavioural changes or physical signs that may indicate exposure to violence at home.

Local safeguarding partnerships, multi-agency forums, and newsletters are invaluable resources for staying up to date on these trends. Attending cluster meetings or participating in safeguarding networks allows practitioners to share information, discuss emerging concerns, and learn from the experiences of other professionals. These opportunities for collaboration ensure that safeguarding practices remain dynamic and responsive to the evolving risks children may face.

Practitioners should also use local data to inform their training and policies. For example, if online exploitation is identified as a growing threat in the community, settings can prioritise training on recognising and responding to digital safeguarding issues. This might include teaching practitioners how to spot signs of grooming, implementing age-appropriate online safety education for children, and engaging parents in conversations about monitoring and managing internet use at home. We know we are talking Early Years but a child is a child under the age of 18.

By combining professional curiosity with an understanding of local safeguarding trends, practitioners can take a proactive, informed approach to protecting children. This dual focus not only enhances the effectiveness of safeguarding practices but also ensures that every child's unique circumstances and risks are considered, creating a safer and more supportive environment for all.

Building Partnerships to Strengthen Safeguarding

Safeguarding is most effective when it's a shared responsibility. Collaboration with parents, outside agencies, and other professionals ensures that children receive holistic protection and support.

Engaging with Parents

Open, respectful communication with parents is a cornerstone of effective safeguarding. Building trust and maintaining open lines of dialogue enable practitioners to develop strong partnerships with families, creating a supportive environment that promotes the well-being of the child. These interactions allow practitioners to gain valuable insights into the child's home life, behaviours and any potential challenges that might impact their safety or development.

Daily touchpoints, such as drop-off and pick-up times, provide informal yet meaningful opportunities to engage with parents. These brief conversations can help practitioners establish rapport, share observations about the child's day, and gently raise any concerns that may have been noticed. For example, a practitioner might mention changes in a child's behaviour, such as increased clinginess or withdrawn tendencies, in a nonconfrontational way that invites collaboration rather than defensiveness.

Formal meetings, such as parent consultations or reviews of individual learning plans, offer a more structured setting for discussing safeguarding concerns. These meetings allow for a deeper exploration of issues and provide space for parents to share their perspectives. Practitioners should approach these discussions with empathy, ensuring parents feel supported while keeping the focus firmly on the child's best interests.

However, it is crucial that practitioners remain vigilant and objective, recognising when concerns need to be escalated. Safeguarding always prioritises the well-being of the child, even if addressing the issue involves difficult or sensitive conversations with families. For instance, if a child discloses information that raises serious concerns, practitioners must act decisively by following the setting's safeguarding procedures and involving the designated safeguarding lead (DSL).

Practitioners should also be mindful of maintaining confidentiality and professionalism when escalating concerns. While open communication with parents is essential, certain situations may require discretion to protect the child and ensure the integrity of the safeguarding process. In these cases, practitioners must balance transparency with the need to act swiftly and appropriately.

By fostering a culture of open, respectful communication, practitioners can build trust with families while ensuring that safeguarding remains the priority. This balanced approach not only strengthens the relationship between home and setting but also ensures that children receive the protection and support they need to thrive.

Collaborating with Outside Agencies

Collaborating with external professionals, such as social workers, health visitors, police, and safeguarding leads, is integral to creating robust safeguarding practices. These partnerships bring specialised expertise, diverse perspectives, and valuable resources that enable early years practitioners to respond effectively to complicated situations and provide holistic support to children and their families.

Safeguarding leads, for example, play a crucial role in guiding settings on how to handle sensitive issues such as disclosures of abuse or neglect. They offer practical advice on the steps to take, ensuring that concerns are escalated appropriately and in accordance with legal and procedural requirements. Their oversight helps practitioners navigate challenging scenarios with confidence, ensuring that children's safety remains the top priority.

Social workers bring a wealth of experience in supporting vulnerable children and families. They can coordinate multi-agency interventions, such as organising child protection conferences or developing child-in-need plans. By working closely with social workers, early years practitioners can ensure that their concerns are acted upon promptly and that families receive the comprehensive support they need to address underlying issues.

Health visitors are another vital partner, particularly when safeguarding concerns are linked to a child's physical or emotional well-being. They can provide insight into a child's developmental history, medical needs, or family dynamics, helping practitioners better understand the context of safeguarding concerns. For example, a health visitor might flag patterns of missed medical appointments as a potential indicator of neglect, prompting early intervention.

Police and other law enforcement professionals are critical allies in addressing safeguarding concerns involving criminal activity, such as domestic abuse, exploitation, or county lines. Initiatives like Operation Encompass demonstrate how timely information-sharing between police and early years settings can mitigate the impact of traumatic events on children. Practitioners working in tandem with police can take proactive steps to ensure children feel safe and supported after witnessing or experiencing distressing incidents.

In addition to providing direct support, external professionals also contribute to the development of safeguarding knowledge and skills within the setting. For instance, they might lead training sessions on recognising specific safeguarding risks, such as online exploitation or radicalisation, equipping staff with the tools to identify and respond to emerging threats.

Collaboration with these agencies fosters a shared approach to safeguarding, ensuring no child or family falls through the cracks. It also reinforces the importance of clear, open communication and the value of a multi-disciplinary perspective in protecting children from harm and supporting their overall well-being.

Inter-Setting Collaboration

Collaborating with other early years settings to share knowledge and best practices is a powerful way to enhance safeguarding processes and maintain high standards across the sector. This collaborative approach fosters a sense of community and shared responsibility, ensuring that every setting benefits from the collective experience and expertise of others.

One effective method of collaboration is attending local safeguarding cluster meetings, where practitioners, safeguarding leads, and other professionals come together to discuss emerging trends, share successful strategies, and address common challenges. These meetings provide valuable opportunities to stay informed about local safeguarding issues, such as increases in domestic abuse, exploitation risks, or specific community concerns. Practitioners can exchange practical ideas and resources to better address these issues within their settings.

Joint training sessions are another key avenue for collaboration. By participating in shared training events, staff from different settings can learn from one another while gaining consistent, high-quality safeguarding knowledge. These sessions ensure that practitioners across the area are aligned in their understanding of policies, procedures, and best practices, which is especially important when children transition between settings or require multi-agency support.

In addition to formal meetings and training, peer mentoring and resource sharing can further strengthen safeguarding efforts. For instance, settings with strong safeguarding processes might mentor those in need of support, providing guidance on policy implementation or staff development. Sharing templates for safeguarding policies, risk assessments, or family engagement strategies can reduce duplication of effort and ensure consistency across settings.

By building a culture of collaboration, early years professionals can collectively raise the standard of safeguarding, ensuring that every child is protected and supported regardless of the setting they attend. This shared approach also reinforces the idea that safeguarding is not just the responsibility of individual practitioners or settings but a collective commitment to the well-being of all children in the community.

Demonstrating Robust Policies

During inspections, safeguarding is invariably a top priority, as it reflects the setting's commitment to protecting children and ensuring their well-being. Inspectors will conduct a thorough evaluation of how effectively your setting safeguards children, focusing on several key areas:

- Implementation

Inspectors will examine whether your safeguarding policies are clear, comprehensive, and aligned with the latest statutory guidance, such as *Keeping Children Safe in Education 2024*. They will assess how these policies are communicated to staff, parents, and other stakeholders and whether they are actively embedded in daily practice rather than existing as mere documentation. Settings must demonstrate that policies are consistently followed and regularly reviewed to address emerging safeguarding challenges.

- Staff Training and Knowledge: A critical aspect of the inspection will be staff awareness and understanding of safeguarding procedures. Inspectors may speak with staff at all levels to assess their ability to recognise signs of abuse, neglect, or exploitation, manage disclosures from children, and escalate concerns appropriately. Practitioners must show confidence in their roles, demonstrating that they know whom to approach—such as the Designated Safeguarding Lead (DSL)—and the steps required for timely intervention.

- Management of Safeguarding Concerns: Inspectors will review how concerns are identified, recorded, and acted upon within the setting. They will evaluate whether concerns are escalated promptly to the DSL or external agencies, such as children's services, and whether records are meticulously kept to provide a clear audit trail. Evidence of follow-up actions, multi-agency collaboration, and support provided to children and families will be scrutinised to ensure that safeguarding is not only reactive but also proactive.

- Safeguarding practices : Inspectors will assess whether safer recruitment protocols are in place and consistently applied. This includes reviewing the processes for conducting DBS checks, verifying references, and ensuring thorough vetting of all staff and volunteers.

- Creating a safeguarding culture: Beyond policies and procedures, inspectors will look for evidence that safeguarding is ingrained in the setting's ethos. This involves observing staff interactions with children, assessing how well children are encouraged to express their feelings or share concerns, and determining whether the environment fosters a sense of safety and respect.

- Operation Encompass & Multi Agency working: If the setting is part of initiatives like Operation Encompass, inspectors will examine how effectively these are integrated into safeguarding practices. They will look for evidence of collaboration with external agencies and how information sharing enhances the protection of children.

By demonstrating robust safeguarding practices that are consistently applied and effectively communicated, settings can provide inspectors with the assurance that children's safety is their highest priority. This comprehensive approach not only ensures compliance but also builds trust with families and stakeholders, reinforcing the setting's reputation as a safe and nurturing environment.

Staff Confidence and Knowledge

Inspectors will likely speak with staff to assess their understanding of safeguarding. Practitioners should confidently explain how they recognise signs of abuse, manage disclosures, and escalate concerns. Regular training ensures that all staff are prepared for this aspect of the inspection.

Evidence of Safe Practices

Documentation, such as risk assessments, training records, and incident logs, provides tangible evidence of safeguarding efforts. Demonstrating how concerns are recorded and followed up shows that the setting prioritises children's safety.

The Impact of Effective Safeguarding

When safeguarding is done well, it creates an environment where children can grow, learn, and thrive without fear. They feel valued, supported, and confident, knowing that the adults around them are there to protect and nurture them.

For parents, effective safeguarding provides reassurance that their children are in safe hands. It builds trust in the setting and strengthens the partnership between home and early years care.

For practitioners, a strong safeguarding culture fosters confidence, clarity, and a shared sense of purpose. It equips them to handle challenges with professionalism and compassion, ensuring that every decision is made in the best interest of the child.

T is for Training

Empowering Staff for Excellence

Training is paramount in an early years setting. It equips staff with the knowledge, skills, and confidence to deliver outstanding care and education while fostering their professional growth and satisfaction. A well-trained team isn't just better at meeting the needs of children; they are also more motivated, collaborative, and reflective in their practice. Training isn't a one-off event—it's an ongoing journey. The best settings embed continuous professional development (CPD) into their culture, ensuring that staff are always learning, adapting, and improving. From mandatory courses to specialist training and peer learning, investing in staff development is an investment in the quality of care provided.

Certain training topics are fundamental for ensuring compliance, safety, and high standards. Mandatory courses such as safeguarding, paediatric first aid, food hygiene, and health and safety are non-negotiable. Safeguarding training ensures that staff are confident in recognising and responding to concerns, while first aid training equips them to handle emergencies effectively.

Food hygiene training helps maintain safe practices in meal preparation, particularly in settings catering to children with allergies, and health and safety training ensures risks are managed effectively to create a secure environment for all.

Specialist training allows staff to deepen their expertise and meet the diverse needs of the children in their care. For example, training in special educational needs and disabilities (SEND) equips staff to support children with specific challenges, such as autism or sensory processing needs. Behaviour support training provides strategies for managing challenging behaviours constructively, helping to create a calm and supportive atmosphere. Outdoor learning courses, such as forest school training, enable practitioners to make the most of outdoor spaces, balancing safety with opportunities for exploration and risk-taking. Together, these specialised areas enhance staff confidence and ensure that every child's individual needs are met.

Understanding the Early Years Foundation Stage (EYFS) framework is also critical. Staff must be confident in planning, observing, and assessing in line with EYFS requirements while ensuring activities remain engaging and child-centred. For example, practitioners should know how to use play to support the seven areas of learning and development, tailoring their approach to each child's interests and developmental stage. This understanding ensures that the curriculum is not only followed but brought to life in ways that inspire and engage.

Continuous professional development is about fostering a culture of learning and growth. Peer learning is a powerful way to achieve this. Encouraging staff to share best practices, observe one another, and collaborate on strategies creates a dynamic, supportive environment where everyone can grow. For example, a team member who recently attended training on sensory play might lead a workshop for colleagues, sharing practical ideas and insights. Regular reflection is another key component of professional development. Through appraisals and supervision meetings, staff can reflect on their strengths, identify areas for improvement, and set personal goals. This process helps individuals take ownership of their learning journey and ensures that their development aligns with the needs of the setting.

Leadership plays a vital role in embedding training into the culture of a setting. Managers should create a clear training plan, outlining schedules for renewing mandatory courses, budgets for external workshops, and opportunities for in-house learning. By regularly reviewing and updating the plan, leaders can ensure that training remains relevant and aligned with the setting's goals. Empowering staff to take ownership of their development further enhances engagement. Providing access to online courses or a resource library allows team members to explore topics of interest at their own pace, bringing fresh ideas and perspectives to the group.

Collaborating with external organisations, other settings, and even parents can enrich training opportunities. Partnerships with local training providers ensure access to high-quality, sector-specific courses, such as those offered by safeguarding boards or early years networks. Networking with other settings allows for shared training sessions, reducing costs and fostering collaboration. For example, a group of settings might organise a joint workshop on outdoor learning, benefiting from shared resources and expertise. Parents can also be valuable contributors to staff development. For instance, a parent who is a speech therapist might lead a session on language development, offering practical, real-world insights while strengthening the partnership between home and setting.

Training is more than a requirement—it's a cornerstone of everything we do in early years education. By prioritising CPD, fostering collaboration, and encouraging reflection, settings create a motivated, knowledgeable team that's ready to meet the needs of every child. When training is embedded into daily practice, it becomes more than a professional obligation; it becomes a source of pride, inspiration, and continuous growth for the entire team. Through ongoing development, practitioners can confidently provide the highest standard of care and education, ensuring that every child thrives in their early years environment.

U is Understanding Needs

Supporting Every Child's Individual Journey

Understanding the needs of each child in your setting is fundamental to delivering high-quality early years education and care. Every child is unique, with their own strengths, challenges, interests, and developmental pathways. By taking the time to understand these needs, practitioners can provide tailored support that helps each child thrive. This understanding goes beyond surface-level observations; it requires empathy, active listening, collaboration with families, and an awareness of external factors that may influence a child's development.

Understanding needs also plays a key role in inspections, as it demonstrates that your setting is truly child-centred. Inspectors will look at how well you know the children in your care and how this knowledge informs your planning, interactions, and support strategies.

Why Understanding Needs Matters

Children enter early years settings with diverse experiences, developmental stages, and cultural backgrounds. Some may need additional support to develop language skills, while others may be navigating challenges like changes at home or special educational needs and disabilities (SEND). Understanding these individual needs is crucial for several reasons:

Promoting Equality: Understanding each child's needs ensures that all children have equal opportunities to participate, learn, and succeed, regardless of their starting point.

Supporting Well-Being:When practitioners understand what children need to feel safe and secure, they can create environments where children are happy and confident.

Maximising Learning Opportunities:T ailoring activities to children's needs ensures they are challenged appropriately, helping them achieve their potential.

How to Understand Children's Needs

Understanding needs requires a multi-faceted approach that combines observations, communication, and collaboration.

Observing Children Closely

Observations are a powerful tool for understanding children's needs. By watching how children play, interact, and respond to their environment, practitioners can gain insights into their interests, abilities, and challenges.

For example, if a child consistently chooses solitary play, this might indicate a preference for independent activities or a need for support in developing social skills. By recognising this, practitioners can plan activities that gently encourage peer interaction while respecting the child's preferences.

Listening to Children

Children often express their needs through their words, actions, and emotions. Practitioners should actively listen to children, creating opportunities for them to share their thoughts and feelings. This might involve:

-   Asking open-ended questions, such as, "What do you think about this activity?"
-   Providing visual aids or prompts to help non-verbal children communicate.
-   Responding with empathy and validating their emotions.
-   Children's Voices and Children's Choices

For example, a child expressing frustration during a group activity might indicate that they feel overwhelmed. By listening and observing, practitioners can adapt the activity or provide additional support.

Partnering with Parents

Parents are an invaluable source of information about their children's needs. Regular communication with families helps practitioners build a holistic understanding of each child, incorporating insights from home as well as the setting.

This might involve:

-   Daily handovers where parents can share updates or concerns.
-   Regular parent meetings to discuss progress and goals.

- Inviting parents to share cultural practices or traditions that are important to their family.

For instance, if a parent shares that their child struggles with transitions at home, practitioners can use this information to plan smoother transitions within the setting, such as using visual timetables or preparing the child in advance for changes.

Collaborating with Professionals

Some children may have additional needs that require support from external professionals, such as speech therapists, educational psychologists, or special educational needs coordinators (SENCOs). Working closely with these specialists ensures that children receive tailored interventions that address their specific challenges.

For example, a child with delayed speech might benefit from strategies suggested by a speech therapist, such as using picture cards or modelling simple phrases during play.

Tailoring Support to Individual Needs

Once you understand a child's needs, the next step is to tailor your support accordingly.

Adapting Activities and Resources

Practitioners should ensure that activities and resources are inclusive and accessible to all children. This might involve:

- Providing sensory materials for children with sensory processing needs.
- Breaking tasks into smaller, manageable steps for children who find longer activities challenging.
- Offering bilingual resources or visual aids for children with English as an additional language (EAL).

For example, a child with fine motor challenges might benefit from activities that strengthen their hand muscles, such as threading beads or playing with dough.

Creating a Flexible Environment

An understanding of needs should inform the physical and emotional environment of the setting. For instance:

- Quiet corners or sensory areas can provide a retreat for children who feel overwhelmed.
- Flexible seating arrangements can accommodate children who need more space or prefer standing while working.
- Visual cues, such as picture schedules, help children who need additional support with routines.

Encouraging Peer Relationships

Understanding social needs is just as important as understanding developmental milestones. Practitioners can support children in building relationships by:

- Pairing them with peers who have similar interests.
- Facilitating group activities that encourage collaboration.
- Modelling positive interactions and conflict resolution skills.

For instance, if a child struggles to join group play, practitioners might create small-group activities that provide a less intimidating environment for social interaction.

The Role of Understanding Needs in Inspections

During inspections, Ofsted will assess how well you understand and meet the needs of the children in your care. This involves:

Evidence of Individualised Planning

Inspectors will look at how observations and assessments inform planning. They'll want to see that activities are tailored to children's individual needs and interests, rather than being one-size-fits-all.

For example, planning might show that a child who loves dinosaurs is supported with dino-themed activities across learning areas, from counting dinosaur footprints (maths) to creating a dinosaur habitat (creative play).

Partnerships with Parents and Professionals

Strong partnerships with families and external professionals demonstrate your commitment to meeting children's needs. Inspectors may ask how you engage parents in their child's learning or how you work with specialists to support children with SEND.

For instance, evidence of regular parent meetings, shared learning journals, or collaborative strategies with a SENCO highlights your proactive approach.

Inclusive Practice

Inspectors will evaluate how inclusive your setting is, considering whether all children feel valued and supported. This includes looking at:

- The accessibility of your environment and resources.
- How you celebrate diversity and cultural differences.
- Strategies for supporting children with additional needs.

V is for Vision

Setting a Direction for Growth and Excellence

Your vision is the heartbeat of your early years setting—it defines what you stand for, shapes your ethos, and sets the tone for everything you do. A clear, well-communicated vision is more than just a statement on a website or policy document; it's the guiding force behind your daily practices, long-term strategy, and the experiences you create for children, families, and staff.

A strong vision does not emerge overnight. It is crafted with intention, reflecting the values, goals, and aspirations of everyone involved in your setting. This clarity of purpose inspires confidence in parents, provides staff with a shared sense of direction, and ensures that every child benefits from a cohesive, nurturing approach to learning and care. With a robust vision, a setting becomes more than just a place—it transforms into a community of growth, support and excellence.

Creating and Communicating Your Vision

The most effective visions are rooted in deeply held values that resonate with your team, families, and the wider community. Crafting and communicating this vision is a collaborative process that lays the groundwork for a united and inspired setting.

Values-Led Approach

The foundation of any strong vision is a clear understanding of your values. Begin by asking fundamental questions: What do we stand for? What do we hope to achieve for the children in our care? These values should reflect the unique strengths and priorities of your setting, whether it's fostering creativity, championing inclusivity, building resilience, or creating a love for outdoor learning.

For instance, if your setting values independence, your vision might highlight the importance of creating an environment where children are empowered to explore, make choices, and grow at their own pace. Similarly, a setting with a strong emphasis on sustainability might craft a vision centred around eco-friendly practices and connecting children with nature.

This values-led approach isn't about ticking boxes for inspections—it's about defining principles that will shape every decision, policy, and interaction in your setting. It ensures that the choices you make are purposeful and aligned with your broader goals.

Shared Goals

Your vision shouldn't come solely from the leadership team; it should be a collective effort shaped by the voices of staff, parents, and even the children themselves. Involving your community ensures that your vision reflects shared aspirations and creates a sense of ownership among stakeholders.

Workshops, brainstorming sessions, or surveys can be valuable tools for gathering input. For instance, staff workshops might explore what makes the setting special, while parents could share their hopes for their children's experiences. Including children in the process—through artwork, stories, or simple conversations—can add a meaningful layer to your vision, capturing their perspective on what makes the setting a happy and inspiring place.

Once your vision is defined, communicate it widely and consistently. Display it prominently in your setting, include it in newsletters and welcome packs, and reference it during team meetings and training sessions. The more visible and regularly discussed your vision is, the more it becomes a living, breathing part of your setting's identity.

Embedding the Vision

Crafting a vision is one thing; ensuring it becomes the foundation of your daily practices is where its true power lies. A vision is only meaningful when it actively guides decisions, policies, and interactions within the setting.

Your vision should influence every aspect of your setting, from the environment you create to the activities you plan. For instance, if your vision emphasises outdoor learning, you might invest in rich outdoor spaces, incorporate nature-based activities into your curriculum, and train staff in forest school principles.

Translate your vision into actionable steps by breaking it down into specific goals and strategies.

For example, if inclusivity is central to your ethos, ensure that:

Resources reflect diverse cultures, abilities, and experiences.

Policies actively promote equal opportunities.

Staff receive training to support children with additional needs.

Reflect regularly on how well your vision is being implemented. Are staff embracing it in their interactions with children and families? Are your policies and procedures aligned with it? Tools like staff appraisals, parent feedback, and team discussions can help evaluate whether your vision is consistently influencing practice. Adjustments can then be made to ensure it remains an active and integral part of your setting.

Your vision isn't just an internal compass—it's also a vital tool for engaging parents, carers, and the wider community. Demonstrating how your vision informs decisions, such as introducing new activities or redesigning spaces, fosters transparency and trust.

For example, if your vision prioritises creativity, you could share stories of how children are encouraged to explore art, music, and role play. Social media updates, newsletters, or open days can highlight these initiatives, helping families understand the "why" behind your actions.

A well-embedded vision also simplifies recruitment. Prospective staff who align with your values are more likely to be drawn to your setting, ensuring a cohesive team committed to delivering on your shared goals.

Adapting and Evolving Your Vision

While a vision provides stability and direction, it should also be flexible enough to evolve with your setting's needs. As your community changes, or as new educational research emerges, your vision should be revisited to ensure it remains relevant and impactful.

Responding to Community Needs

Changes in the local community can significantly influence your vision. For instance, if your area sees an increase in families from diverse cultural backgrounds, your vision might shift to emphasise celebrating cultural diversity and supporting bilingual learners. Similarly, if environmental awareness becomes a pressing concern, incorporating sustainability into your vision could reflect the growing importance of eco-friendly practices.

Continuous Improvement

Reviewing your vision regularly is essential to ensure it remains relevant, meaningful, and aligned with the evolving needs of your setting. A vision is not a static declaration; it is a dynamic framework that should grow and adapt alongside changes in your community, educational priorities, and the needs of the children and families you serve.

Involving your team in this process is key to fostering a sense of connection and ownership. When staff contribute to shaping and refining the vision, they are more likely to embrace it wholeheartedly and incorporate it into their daily practice. For instance, annual staff meetings or dedicated vision workshops can provide opportunities to reflect on how the vision is being realised. During these sessions, practitioners can share observations, celebrate successes, and identify areas for improvement.

Discussions might explore questions like:

- How well is our vision reflected in our environment, activities, and interactions with children?
- Are there specific challenges that prevent us from fully realising our vision?
- What new opportunities or community changes should influence our vision moving forward?

Gathering input from across the team also allows for diverse perspectives, ensuring that the vision captures the collective aspirations of the setting. Additionally, inviting feedback from parents, carers, and even children can provide valuable insights into how the vision is perceived and where it could evolve to better meet the needs of the community.

This regular review process keeps your vision dynamic, rather than allowing it to become a static or outdated statement. By actively revisiting and refining your vision, you ensure that it remains an inspiring and guiding force for everyone involved, helping your setting stay forward-thinking, child-centred, and aligned with its goals for excellence and growth.

Your vision plays a critical role during inspections, as it demonstrates the direction and purpose behind your setting's approach to early years education. Inspectors will look for evidence that your vision isn't just aspirational—it should be visible in your practices, policies, and environment.

Be prepared to clearly articulate your vision and explain how it shapes your approach. For example, if your vision focuses on fostering independence, describe how your environment supports self-directed learning, such as through accessible resources or activities that encourage problem-solving.

Inspectors will also assess whether your vision aligns with the EYFS framework and statutory requirements. Ensure that your policies, procedures, and practices reflect your vision while meeting regulatory standards. For example, if sustainability is part of your vision, highlight eco-friendly policies like recycling initiatives or nature-based learning activities.

Providing evidence of how your vision impacts children's outcomes—for instance, through progress tracking or parent testimonials—can further demonstrate its value during inspections.

The Impact of a Strong Vision

A clear and well-communicated vision transforms an early years setting, creating a shared sense of purpose that drives excellence across all areas.

For children, a strong vision ensures consistency and focus in their care and learning experiences. When staff are united by a shared ethos, children benefit from an environment that is nurturing, stimulating, and aligned with their developmental needs.

For staff, a clear vision fosters motivation and direction. Knowing they are part of a team working toward a common goal enhances job satisfaction and empowers them to contribute meaningfully to the setting's success.

For parents and carers, a well-implemented vision inspires trust and confidence. Families feel reassured knowing their children are in a setting guided by strong values and a commitment to excellence.

A Vision for Excellence and Growth

A strong vision is the foundation for everything a setting achieves. It shapes the culture, drives innovation, and ensures that every decision is rooted in what's best for children. More than just a statement of intent, a vision is a commitment—to children, families, and staff—to continually strive for excellence.

In early years education, where every interaction and decision matters, a clear and dynamic vision ensures that your setting remains focused, forward-thinking, and child-centred. It is the compass that guides your journey, creating a place where children can flourish, families feel supported, and staff are inspired to deliver their very best.

By embedding, evolving, and championing your vision, you create a legacy of growth and excellence that resonates far beyond the walls of your setting.

W is for Well-being

Supporting the Physical and Emotional Health of Children and Staff

Well-being is at the heart of every thriving early years setting. When children and staff feel safe, valued, and supported, they're more likely to flourish, both emotionally and physically. Prioritising well-being isn't just about creating a happy environment—it's about building resilience, fostering strong relationships, and nurturing a sense of belonging that benefits everyone in the setting.

For children, well-being lays the foundation for healthy development, helping them build the confidence and emotional regulation skills they need to explore the world. For staff, it's about creating a positive, supportive workplace culture where they feel motivated and empowered to deliver their best. By embedding well-being into the ethos of your setting, you create a community where everyone feels cared for and valued.

Promoting Children's Well-Being

Supporting children's well-being involves addressing both their emotional and physical needs. These are deeply interconnected—when children feel emotionally secure, they're more likely to engage in activities that support their physical health, and vice versa.

Emotional Security

Children thrive when they feel safe, loved, and valued. Building strong relationships with key workers is central to fostering this emotional security. A trusted adult provides a consistent source of comfort and encouragement, helping children feel confident as they navigate new experiences. This bond also makes it easier for practitioners to identify when something might be wrong, whether a child is struggling with separation anxiety or has experienced a significant change at home.

Creating a nurturing environment where children are listened to and respected further enhances their sense of security. For example, incorporating opportunities for children to share their thoughts and feelings during circle time helps them feel heard and valued. Visual aids like emotion charts can also help children express themselves, particularly if they're not yet confident with verbal communication.

Physical Activity

Movement is a powerful way to support both physical and emotional well-being. Daily opportunities for physical activity—whether it's running in the outdoor play area, climbing on equipment, or participating in dance and yoga sessions—help children build strength, coordination, and confidence. Physical activity also reduces stress and promotes the release of endorphins, boosting mood and energy levels.

Incorporating physical activity into your routine doesn't have to be complicated. Even simple activities like obstacle courses, nature walks, or group games like "What's the Time, Mr. Wolf?" provide opportunities for children to move their bodies while developing social skills and teamwork.

Mindfulness Activities

Teaching children mindfulness from an early age helps them develop tools for managing their emotions and staying present in the moment. Activities like breathing exercises, quiet reading, or sensory play can help children regulate their emotions and feel calmer during transitions or after periods of high energy.

For instance, a "calm corner" stocked with soft cushions, books, and sensory items like stress balls or textured fabrics can provide a retreat for children who feel overwhelmed. Practitioners can also guide children through simple breathing exercises, such as "balloon breaths," where they imagine inflating and deflating a balloon with each inhale and exhale.

Supporting Staff Well-Being

While children's well-being is often the primary focus, staff well-being is equally important. A happy, healthy team is better equipped to meet the needs of the children and create a positive atmosphere. Supporting staff well-being means fostering a workplace culture that values and prioritises mental health, inclusion, and professional growth.

Workplace Culture

A positive workplace culture is built on trust, respect, and collaboration. Staff should feel that their contributions are valued and that their voices are heard. Regular team meetings, open-door policies, and opportunities for staff to share feedback or suggestions all help create an inclusive and supportive environment.

Encouraging teamwork and mutual support also strengthens relationships within the team. For example, pairing experienced staff with newer team members for mentoring can build confidence and create a sense of camaraderie. Celebrating team successes, such as achieving a positive inspection or completing a challenging project, fosters a collective sense of pride and achievement.

Mental Health Support

The demands of working in early years education can be challenging, and it's essential to provide resources that support staff mental health. This might include offering access to counselling services, creating a mental health policy, or providing information on managing stress and burnout.

Regular check-ins with staff provide opportunities to discuss any concerns and offer tailored support. For example, a practitioner who feels overwhelmed by their workload might benefit from adjustments to their responsibilities or additional training to build confidence in certain areas.

Recognition and Reward

Showing appreciation for staff contributions goes a long way in boosting morale and motivation. This doesn't have to be costly—a simple "thank you" or acknowledging someone's efforts during a team meeting can make a significant impact.

More formal recognition, such as "employee of the month" schemes, professional development opportunities, or small rewards like gift cards, further demonstrates that staff are valued. Celebrating milestones, such as work anniversaries or completing training courses, adds a personal touch that helps staff feel seen and appreciated.

Embedding Well-Being in Daily Practice

Well-being isn't a standalone initiative—it should be woven into every aspect of your setting's culture and operations.

For Children

Embed well-being into your routines by incorporating activities that support both physical and emotional health. For example:

- Start the day with a group activity that sets a positive tone, such as singing a welcome song or sharing something they're looking forward to.
- Provide structured opportunities for mindfulness, like a daily quiet time or guided relaxation session.
- Encourage peer relationships through group games and collaborative projects that teach teamwork and empathy.

For Staff

Ensure that staff well-being is part of your leadership strategy. This might include:

- Regular one-to-one meetings to check in on their workload and overall well-being.
- Offering flexibility where possible, such as accommodating personal commitments or providing time for training and reflection.
- Creating spaces where staff can relax during breaks, with comfortable seating, refreshments, and minimal distractions.

Partnerships to Support Well-Being

Collaborating with parents, local agencies, and external organisations can enhance your approach to well-being.

Parents are key partners in promoting children's well-being. Regular communication about their child's emotional and physical health helps create a consistent approach between home and the setting. For example, sharing strategies for managing emotions or encouraging active play at home can reinforce the work being done in the setting.

Workshops or resources for parents, such as sessions on mindfulness techniques or healthy meal planning, further strengthen this partnership and provide valuable tools for supporting children's well-being outside the setting.

Working with External Agencies

Local agencies and organisations can provide valuable support for both children and staff. For example, mental health charities might offer counselling or training on resilience, while sports coaches or yoga instructors can lead physical activities. Collaborating with these partners broadens the resources available and enhances the overall well-being offering.

Well-Being and Inspections

During inspections, well-being will be a key focus. Inspectors will want to see how your setting supports the physical and emotional health of both children and staff.

Be prepared to demonstrate how well-being is embedded into your daily routines and activities. For example, show how mindfulness activities help children manage emotions, or provide evidence of how outdoor play supports physical health. Sharing examples of how you've supported individual children, such as helping a child settle into the setting or managing transitions, highlights your commitment to well-being.

Provide evidence of your staff well-being initiatives, such as policies, training, or feedback mechanisms. For example, you might share how regular appraisals include discussions about well-being or how access to mental health support has benefited the team. Highlighting a positive workplace culture and strong relationships within the team further demonstrates that staff well-being is a priority.

The Impact of Prioritising Well-Being

When well-being is prioritised, the benefits ripple outward. Children who feel emotionally and physically supported are more confident, resilient, and ready to learn. They develop positive relationships with peers and practitioners, building the foundations for lifelong social and emotional skills.

For staff, a focus on well-being creates a happier, more motivated team. Practitioners who feel valued and supported are more likely to stay in their roles, reducing turnover and ensuring continuity of care for children. A positive workplace culture also fosters collaboration, innovation and a shared sense of purpose.

X is for eXemplary Practice

Striving for the Highest Standards in Care and Education

Exemplary practice is about going above and beyond in every aspect of your setting. It's not just about meeting expectations—it's about exceeding them in ways that inspire children, families, and your team. It means setting exceptional standards in care and education, embedding a culture of excellence, and ensuring that your setting is a place where children thrive and staff feel proud of their work.

Exemplary practice doesn't happen by chance. It requires intentionality, innovation and an ongoing commitment to reflection and improvement. It's about creating a setting where every child feels seen, valued, and inspired, where families feel confident and supported, and where staff are motivated to deliver their best.

Achieving and maintaining exemplary practice means focusing on the areas that truly make a difference to children and their families.

Child-Centred Learning

At the heart of exemplary practice is the child. Every activity, interaction, and decision should be rooted in the needs and interests of the children in your care. This means tailoring your curriculum to reflect their passions and developmental stages, creating an environment where they can explore, question, and learn in their own unique way.

For example, if a group of children shows an interest in transport, you might create role-play opportunities with a train station setup, introduce books about vehicles, or organise a visit to a local bus depot. By following their interests, you create a sense of ownership and engagement that drives deeper learning.

A rich, engaging curriculum also ensures that all areas of the Early Years Foundation Stage (EYFS) are supported. From outdoor adventures that promote physical development to storytelling sessions that build communication and language skills, your activities should cater to the whole child.

Innovative Approaches

Exemplary practice means staying ahead of the curve. By keeping up-to-date with new research, pedagogical approaches, and sector developments, you can continuously improve the experiences you offer. This might involve incorporating elements of forest school principles, experimenting with loose parts play, or introducing mindfulness activities to support emotional regulation.

Innovation doesn't have to mean reinventing the wheel—it can be as simple as trying a new approach to group time, introducing open-ended resources, or collaborating with outside organisations to bring fresh ideas into your setting.

Inclusion and Diversity

An inclusive setting is a thriving setting. Exemplary practice means ensuring that every child feels valued, supported, and celebrated for who they are. This includes reflecting the diversity of your community in your resources, activities, and environment, and providing additional support to children with special educational needs and disabilities (SEND).

For example, your setting might feature books and toys that represent different cultures, family structures, and abilities, or host celebrations of festivals from around the world. For children with SEND, exemplary practice might involve using adaptive resources, implementing visual timetables, or working closely with specialists to meet their individual needs.

Showcasing Excellence

Exemplary practice isn't just about doing great things—it's about demonstrating them. Sharing and documenting your achievements helps inspire others, strengthens trust with families, and provides evidence of your commitment to quality.

Documentation

Keeping detailed records is essential for showcasing exemplary practice. This includes documenting children's progress, highlighting how activities are tailored to their interests, and recording feedback from families. For example, a child's learning journey might include photos of them exploring a sensory activity, quotes from their reflections, and notes on how this links to their developmental goals.

Innovative activities can also be documented to show how you're pushing boundaries and trying new approaches. Whether it's a new way of organising your outdoor space or a creative art project inspired by a child's idea, capturing these moments demonstrates your dedication to continuous improvement.

Staff Engagement

Your team is the driving force behind exemplary practice. Empowering staff to lead by example, share ideas, and take ownership of their roles creates a culture of excellence. Encourage staff to attend training, experiment with new approaches, and reflect on their practice.

For instance, a practitioner who's passionate about outdoor learning might take the lead in transforming your outdoor area, introducing bug hunts, gardening activities, or natural play spaces. Recognising and celebrating these contributions helps inspire others and creates a positive, motivated team.

Embedding Exemplary Practice in Daily Practice

Exemplary practice isn't a one-off—it's a daily commitment. By embedding excellence into the culture of your setting, you ensure that high standards are consistently maintained.

For children

For children, exemplary practice means creating an environment where they feel safe, inspired, and supported to take risks and try new things. This could involve:

- Designing spaces that encourage exploration, such as sensory corners or loose parts areas.
- Offering open-ended activities that spark creativity and critical thinking.
- Using positive reinforcement to build confidence and resilience.

For Families

Families are an integral part of exemplary practice. Building strong, trusting relationships with parents and carers ensures consistency between home and the setting. Regular communication, such as newsletters, workshops, or progress meetings, keeps families informed and engaged.

Involving parents in your practice also strengthens their connection to the setting. For example, inviting them to share their cultural traditions or participate in activities creates a sense of community and enriches children's experiences.

For Staff

Staff need to feel valued and supported to deliver exemplary practice. Providing opportunities for training, reflection, and collaboration ensures that your team stays motivated and skilled. Encourage staff to take ownership of their professional development and share their passions with the team.

A positive workplace culture, where staff feel appreciated and inspired, is the foundation of excellence. Simple gestures like recognising achievements, offering flexibility, or providing a comfortable break space can make a big difference.

The Ripple Effect of Exemplary Practice

When you commit to exemplary practice, the benefits ripple out across your setting. Children thrive in an environment where they feel valued and inspired, building the confidence and skills they need for the future. Families feel reassured, knowing their children are receiving the best possible care and education. Staff feel motivated and proud, knowing they're making a difference and contributing to a culture of excellence.

Exemplary practice isn't about being perfect—it's about striving for continuous improvement, embracing innovation, and putting children at the centre of everything you do. By embedding this ethos into your setting, you create a place where everyone—children, families, and staff—can achieve their full potential.

In early years education, where every moment matters, exemplary practice is the key to making a lasting impact. It's what transforms a good setting into a great one, inspiring confidence, curiosity, and joy in everyone who walks through your doors.

Y is for Year-round Preparation

Inspection-Ready Every Day

In the world of early years education, inspections often feel like a looming event on the horizon. However, the secret to a smooth inspection isn't a last-minute scramble—it's maintaining high standards all year round. Year-round preparation ensures that your setting is consistently delivering quality care and education, not just in the run-up to an inspection but every single day.

When readiness becomes part of your daily routine, inspections shift from being a source of stress to a celebration of your hard work and dedication. It's about embedding excellence into your culture, ensuring that your setting operates with integrity and confidence at all times.

Embedding Readiness into Daily Practice

Being inspection-ready isn't about occasional bursts of effort—it's about building habits and systems that ensure quality is always front and centre.

Daily Reflective Practice

Reflection should be part of your everyday routine. Encouraging staff to regularly evaluate their practice, identify successes, and address challenges creates a culture of continuous improvement. For example, you might set aside time at the end of each day for practitioners to share what went well and what could be improved. These quick reflections can highlight small changes that make a big difference, such as rearranging a play area to improve flow or adjusting routines to better meet children's needs.

Documenting these reflections not only helps track progress but also provides evidence for inspectors of how your setting prioritises improvement. Keep a simple log of team discussions, actions taken, and outcomes achieved to show how reflective practice drives your approach.

Regular Updates to Policies and Procedures

Policies and procedures are the backbone of your setting, and they should always be up-to-date and relevant. Year-round preparation means reviewing these documents regularly, not just when an inspection is looming.

Set a schedule for policy reviews—perhaps monthly or quarterly—ensuring that updates reflect current legislation, guidance, and the evolving needs of your setting. For example, if new safeguarding protocols are introduced, update your safeguarding policy promptly and ensure all staff are aware of the changes.

Involve your team in these reviews. Practitioners on the ground often have valuable insights into how policies translate into practice, and their input can help make documents more practical and user-friendly.

Seamless Documentation

Good documentation is at the heart of inspection readiness. From learning journeys to risk assessments, every record should tell the story of how your setting operates at its best. The key is to keep documentation up-to-date and well-organised so that it's easy to access and present when needed.

For example, regularly review children's learning journeys to ensure they accurately reflect progress and next steps. Keep risk assessments current by revisiting them after significant changes, such as introducing new equipment or rearranging spaces. When documentation is integrated into your daily routine, it becomes a natural part of your workflow rather than a daunting task.

Inspection Practice Runs

The thought of an inspector walking through your doors can feel intimidating, but preparation helps turn nerves into confidence. Regularly practising for inspections ensures that everyone knows what to expect and feels ready to showcase their best work.

Quality Improvement Audits.

Conducting quality improvement audits is a powerful way to identify strengths and areas for improvement. You might take turns having different team members act as the "inspector," walking through the setting with a checklist and noting observations. This exercise not only highlights practical issues, like cluttered areas or incomplete documentation, but also helps staff get comfortable answering inspection-style questions.

For example, during an audit, you could ask questions like, "How do you promote inclusivity in your daily practice?" or "What would you do if a child disclosed a safeguarding concern?" Practising these scenarios helps staff articulate their responses confidently when the real inspection happens.

Audits should be constructive and collaborative, focusing on learning and improvement rather than criticism. Use the findings to create action plans that address any gaps, and celebrate the areas where your setting shines.

Building Staff Confidence

A key part of inspection readiness is ensuring that every member of your team feels confident in their role. This doesn't mean memorising policies word-for-word—it's about understanding how their daily work contributes to the setting's overall quality.

Encourage staff to reflect on their strengths and achievements, whether it's their creative approach to planning activities or their ability to build strong relationships with families. Recognising these contributions boosts morale and helps practitioners feel prepared to share their experiences with inspectors.

Providing opportunities for training and professional development also builds confidence. For example, a session on the inspection framework or role-playing common inspection questions can demystify the process and help staff feel more at ease.

Creating a Culture of Excellence

Year-round preparation isn't just about ticking boxes—it's about embedding a culture of excellence into every aspect of your setting.

High Standards Every Day

When excellence becomes the norm, inspection readiness is a natural by-product. This means consistently delivering high-quality care and education, even on the busiest or most challenging days. For example, maintaining a calm, engaging environment during transitions or adapting activities to meet individual needs demonstrates your commitment to quality at all times.

Encourage staff to take pride in their work and approach each day as an opportunity to make a positive impact. Whether it's through creative planning, thoughtful interactions, or collaborative problem-solving, these small, consistent efforts create a setting that's always ready to shine.

Empowering Staff

Empowered staff are paramount of a successful setting. Give your team the tools, training, and support they need to excel in their roles. This might include regular one-to-one meetings, opportunities to attend external training, or time for peer observations and collaboration.

A confident, knowledgeable team not only ensures high standards but also creates a positive atmosphere that children and families can feel. When practitioners feel valued and supported, they're more likely to go above and beyond in their work.

Engaging Families in Preparation

Families play an important role in your setting's success, and involving them in your journey helps build trust and collaboration.

Regular Communication

Keep families informed about your setting's goals, achievements, and areas for improvement. For example, a monthly newsletter might include updates on new initiatives, reminders about policies, or highlights from children's learning journeys.

Encourage parents to share feedback regularly, whether through surveys, suggestion boxes, or informal conversations. Listening to their perspectives not only helps you improve but also shows inspectors that you value family input.

Parent Partnerships

Strong partnerships with parents demonstrate that your setting is committed to working collaboratively for the benefit of every child. Invite families to participate in activities, workshops, or events that reflect your ethos, such as a gardening day to promote outdoor learning or a storytelling evening to encourage literacy.

When parents are engaged and invested in your setting, they become advocates for the quality of care and education you provide.

Using Inspections as a Learning Opportunity

Rather than viewing inspections as a test, treat them as an opportunity to reflect, learn, and grow.

Inspectors' observations can provide valuable insights into areas for improvement. Approach their feedback with an open mind, using it to strengthen your practice and drive positive change. For example, if an inspector suggests enhancing your outdoor provision, involve your team in brainstorming ideas and creating an action plan.

Celebrating Success

Inspections are also an opportunity to celebrate everything you do well. Use the process to highlight your achievements, showcase innovative approaches, and share the stories that make your setting unique.

The Impact of Year-round Preparation

When year-round preparation becomes part of your culture, the benefits extend far beyond inspections. Children thrive in an environment where high standards are consistently maintained, families feel reassured knowing their children are in capable hands, and staff feel confident and proud of their work.

A setting that prioritises readiness isn't just prepared for inspections—it's prepared for anything. By embedding reflection, collaboration, and continuous improvement into your daily routine, you create a community that's always striving for excellence.

Z is for Zero Tolerance

Setting Non-Negotiable Standards for Safety

In an early years setting, zero tolerance means drawing a firm line in the sand on behaviours, actions, or lapses that compromise safety or professionalism. It's about making sure that the highest standards are upheld, day in and day out, so that every child, family, and staff member feels safe, valued, and respected. There's no room for grey areas when it comes to safeguarding, safety, and professional conduct—it's all or nothing.

Zero tolerance doesn't mean creating a harsh or punitive environment. Quite the opposite—it's about fostering a culture of accountability and trust, where everyone understands the importance of certain non-negotiables. When everyone is on the same page about what's expected and why it matters, it lays the groundwork for a safe and nurturing space where children can thrive and staff can work with confidence.

Key Zero-Tolerance Areas

There are certain areas where lapses are simply not an option. These are the foundations of a well-run, safe, and professional early years setting.

Safeguarding Breaches

Safeguarding is the cornerstone of everything we do—it's non-negotiable. Every child deserves to feel safe and protected, and it's our job to ensure that nothing jeopardises their welfare. That means following safeguarding protocols to the letter, whether it's reporting concerns, adhering to safer recruitment practices, or handling sensitive information responsibly.

If, for example, a team member overhears a disclosure from a child but fails to record and escalate it properly, it's not just a lapse in judgment—it's a failure to uphold the child's right to protection. Such breaches need to be addressed immediately, with clear consequences, to maintain the integrity of your safeguarding culture.

Regular training is key to embedding a zero-tolerance approach to safeguarding. All staff must know exactly what's expected of them, feel confident in spotting and responding to concerns, and understand the seriousness of their responsibilities. Safeguarding is not just about ticking boxes—it's about vigilance, action, and a shared commitment to protecting children.

Health and Safety Neglect

Health and safety might not sound glamorous, but it's the backbone of a safe environment. Risk assessments, hygiene protocols, fire drills—these aren't optional extras; they're essential to keeping everyone in your setting safe. A zero-tolerance approach to health and safety means making sure that every corner of your setting is risk-free, every procedure is followed, and every staff member understands their role in maintaining a safe environment.

For example, if a practitioner fails to check that outdoor play equipment is secure and a child gets hurt, it's not just an accident—it's a preventable issue that could have been avoided with proper diligence. Similarly, if hygiene standards slip, children and staff are at risk of illness. Holding everyone accountable to the highest health and safety standards ensures that these risks are minimised.

Bullying, Harassment, and Discrimination

A zero-tolerance approach also means creating an environment where everyone—children, staff, and families—is treated with respect. Bullying, harassment, and discriminatory behaviour have no place in an early years setting. This applies to interactions between staff, among children, and between families and staff.

For example, if a child or staff member experiences unkind or exclusionary behaviour and it's not addressed promptly and effectively, it creates an unsafe atmosphere for everyone. Tackling these issues head-on with clear policies and consistent consequences reinforces the message that respect and kindness are non-negotiable.

Creating a Culture of Accountability

Zero tolerance isn't just about reacting to breaches—it's about setting expectations clearly from the outset and embedding accountability into your culture.

Clear Communication

The first step is making sure that everyone—staff, families, and even children where appropriate—understands the policies and why they exist. During inductions, team meetings, and regular reviews, take time to explain your zero-tolerance policies, using real-world examples to illustrate what they mean in practice.

For example, you might discuss safeguarding scenarios or role-play conversations around health and safety. Giving staff the chance to explore these issues in a supportive environment helps them understand their responsibilities and feel confident in upholding them.

Consistent Enforcement

Zero tolerance only works if it's applied fairly and consistently. If one breach is ignored or handled lightly, it undermines the entire culture of accountability. It's essential to address all issues promptly, following the same process every time, to maintain trust and integrity.

For example, if a staff member repeatedly fails to complete daily safety checks, they should be reminded of their responsibility, supported in understanding the importance of these checks, and held accountable if the lapses continue. Consistent enforcement doesn't mean being overly harsh—it means being fair, transparent, and committed to the standards you've set.

Embedding Zero Tolerance in Daily Practice

Zero tolerance isn't about putting up posters or writing policies—it's about living those principles every day.

For Children

Children learn by example. When they see adults in their setting consistently modelling respect, safety, and accountability, they internalise those values. For example, practitioners who handle minor conflicts between children with kindness and fairness reinforce the message that bullying or exclusion won't be tolerated.

For Staff

Staff must feel supported and empowered to uphold zero-tolerance policies. Regular training, clear communication, and a positive workplace culture all contribute to this. Staff should know that they can raise concerns without fear of judgment and that their commitment to high standards is recognised and valued.

For Families

Parents and carers should also understand your zero-tolerance approach, particularly around safeguarding, health and safety, and respect. Sharing policies during enrolment and providing regular updates ensures that families are on the same page. It also reassures them that your setting takes these issues seriously.

Zero Tolerance and Inspections

Zero tolerance plays a key role during inspections. Inspectors will want to see evidence that your setting is committed to the highest standards and that these principles are embedded in your culture.

Policy Evidence

Ensure that your zero-tolerance policies are well-documented, up-to-date, and accessible to staff and families. Be prepared to show inspectors how these policies are communicated and enforced.

Examples in Action

Sharing real-life examples of how you've applied zero-tolerance policies demonstrates their effectiveness. For instance, you might describe how you handled a safeguarding concern, addressed a health and safety issue, or resolved a conflict involving discriminatory behaviour.

Staff Understanding

Inspectors may ask staff about their understanding of key policies, particularly safeguarding and health and safety. Regular training and mock inspections ensure that your team can confidently articulate their responsibilities and explain how they uphold the setting's standards.

The Impact of Zero Tolerance

When zero tolerance is embedded in your setting, the impact is profound. Children feel safe, respected, and supported to learn and grow. Families trust that their children are in capable hands and that their concerns will be taken seriously. Staff feel empowered to maintain high standards and take pride in their work.

A zero-tolerance approach doesn't just prevent issues—it creates a positive, proactive culture where safety, respect, and accountability are the norm. It sends a clear message that your setting is committed to excellence in every area, building confidence and trust among everyone involved.

Printed in Great Britain
by Amazon

56288303R00129